Morals in a Immoral Age

EDITOR, JOHNIE SCAGGS, JR.

First Printing, 2012

Second Printing, 2021

2212 Bellevue Rd.
Dublin, GA. 31021
478-279-0754
www.basicbibletruth.org

DEDICATION

This book is dedicated to a dear gospel preacher who has worked for many years converting the lost to the Lord. I speak of brother Wallace Maxwell. Brother Maxwell does not consider himself a scholar but many of us who know him believe he is most certainly a scholar in many ways.

He worked for the Wesconnett church of Christ for 30 years, placing heavy emphasis on personal work. If you were to speak to him, be prepared to talk about personal work, for that is his love. During his time with the Wesconnett church, he paved the way for other ministers to follow him. In doing so, he made our work easier.

He has written 4 books, 3 of them on the subject of evangelism, which is dear to his heart. He has written one book on the elders and the preachers working together.

I personally count him as a dear friend and brother in Christ. He is one who I have gone to in order to seek his wisdom and advice in different matters of the kingdom. His knowledge and wisdom have aided me in some of my choice in my work with the Wesconnett church of Christ.

He loves telling the story of how he came to be a gospel preacher. He also loves telling of all the things which took place at the Wesconnett church of Christ during his time as their minister. I have sat, as well as many others, and listen to him tell the same stories over and over, never telling him we have heard that story before.

Brother Maxwell's wife, Dorothy passed away June 11, 2010 leaving a great void in his life. Though nothing or no one can fill this void as she could, his church family here at Wesconnett has taken care of him.

As of the publication of this book, brother Maxwell is 89 years of age. He stated on his 90th birthday, he would love to preach a sermon on that day. Lord willing, he will be able to do so.

Heaven will rejoice when the mighty soldier Wallace Maxwell comes home, but until then we rejoice that he is still with us and still desires to do personal work.

September 2012

Johnie Scaggs, Jr.

INTRODUCTION

At no other time in the history of our country have we been confronted with such loose morals. We are assailed on every side and there seems to be no end as to the lengths people will go to undermine the morals given to us in the Bible.

It is past time that we stand up and lift up the Word of God and let the world know we will not give in to the ways of the world, but rather, we are going to stay true to the Word of God.

It is our prayer that the things written in this short volume will strengthen you and help to resolve to stand firm in the Word of our Lord.

To the glory of Him

Johnie Scaggs, Jr.

TABLE OF CONTENTS

DOMESTIC VIOLENCE

Ryan Frederick

INTRODUCTION

One of the biggest responsibilities a preacher of God's Word has is to address the common problems of our times that are in conflict with God's will. We certainly need to do our best to stay abreast of the things that are going on in the world that may serve as problems or temptations to those in our congregations. I am reminded of the Old Testament account of David's army and what the Bible says about the sons of Issachar. 1 Chronicles 12:32 says, "And of the children of Issachar, which were men that had understanding of the times, to know what Israel ought to do". The book of Esther, in chapter 1, verse 13 references the "wise men, which knew the times, (for so was the king's manner toward all that knew law and judgment)". As preachers of God's Word, we have a responsibility to know the times that we might be able to help with the "perfecting of the saints" (Eph. 4:12) and to avoid the "wiles" and "fiery darts" of the wicked one (Eph. 6:11-16). Most preachers I know seem to do a pretty good job of handling things such as homosexuality, abortion, drug and alcohol abuse, as well as a slew of other relevant topics. However, there seems to be an "elephant in the room" when it comes to social issues that perhaps does not receive the attention that homosexuality, abortion, adultery, or other issues are receiving. This elephant in the room I am speaking of is the issue of domestic violence.

I do not recall growing up hearing very many lessons geared towards this terrible problem. You may not find any books put out by our brotherhood or the religious world in general on the issue of domestic violence. Why is that? If something affects one out of every four women in this country, isn't it worth talking about? 1 It equally affects the men as well because for every woman who is abused, there must be an abuser. That means that roughly 25% of your congregation is affected by domestic violence. If your congregation is the size of mine (about 200 members), that means fifty of them may be affected by this in some way. That's probably more than would be affected by homosexuality, abortion, or even divorce. Yet, why is this problem not being discussed more than it is? Perhaps we have largely ignored it because we do not always see it with our own eyes. Domestic violence too often happens behind closed doors and is not talked about or even discovered until it is too late. It could be we believe it only exists outside of the church and therefore we do not need to discuss it. Brethren, we need to wake up and take a stand against a problem that is becoming more and more relevant in our world today. We need to sober up and realize domestic violence is occurring even within the walls of the Lord's church.

DEFINING AND UNDERSTANDING DOMESTIC VIOLENCE

I believe one of the problems with domestic violence is a lack of understanding of what it actually entails. Some believe domestic violence only occurs when there is physical abuse such as hitting, kicking, choking, shoving, etc. Domestic violence is defined as so much more than that. Here is a definition of domestic violence given by the National Coalition Against Domestic Violence:

> Domestic violence is the willful intimidation, physical assault, battery, sexual assault, and/or other abusive behavior perpetrated by an intimate partner against another. It is an epidemic affecting individuals in every community, regardless of age, economic status, race, religion, nationality or educational background. Violence

against women is often accompanied by emotionally abusive and controlling behavior, and thus is part of a systematic pattern of dominance and control. Domestic violence results in physical injury, psychological trauma, and sometimes death. The consequences of domestic violence can cross generations and truly last a lifetime. 2

Domestic violence is not just a physical assault. It includes sexual assault, verbal and emotional assault, stalking, intimidation, and even economic deprivation. Some examples of domestic violence include name calling or putdowns, keeping a partner from contacting their family and friends, withholding money, and actual, or threatened, physical harm. Perhaps one of the most widespread, but often ignored abuses, is verbal abuse. One cannot be arrested for putting someone else down or calling them hurtful names. Therefore, this abuse is often allowed to continue.

This conduct and behavior generally all boils down to a power struggle where one tries to make their partner totally dependent upon them. It is really all about control. The U.S. Office on Violence Against Women (OVW) describes domestic violence as a "pattern of abusive behavior in any relationship that is used by one partner to gain or maintain power and control over another intimate partner".3 This power struggle is mostly seen in men abusing women, although at times the reverse could be the case. This certainly seems like a pride and selfishness issue.

AN INCREASING PROBLEM

This problem of domestic violence is not a shrinking problem, but rather a growing one. There are several factors behind this rising trend. One is the simple fact that often times these crimes go unreported and therefore unpunished. Listen to the following finding:

Only approximately one-quarter of all physical assaults, one-fifth of all rapes, and one-half of all stalking perpetuated against females by intimate partners are reported to the police. 4

One who is not punished for a wrongdoing will normally continue with the behavior. The wise King Solomon wrote in Ecclesiastes 8:11, "Because sentence against an evil work is not executed speedily, therefore the heart of the sons of men is fully set in them to do evil." The book of Hebrews explains to us the reasoning behind punishment. For those who receive discipline (or chastening) it "yieldeth the peaceable fruit of righteousness unto them which are exercised thereby" (Heb. 12:5-11). Those who do not receive this chastening or punishment will simply continue in the same pattern of behavior until someone, or something, stops or corrects them. Since so many do not report these actions, those guilty of the acts continue their abusive ways.

Another reason why domestic violence is a growing trend is because it is being passed on to younger generations as acceptable behavior. Many young boys and men today wear their white tank top undershirts and call them "wife beaters" as slang. Television and movies have shown men who are perceived as being "cool" both physically and verbally abusing women. This glamorization has given young boys the idea that this is how they should behave. For many young men growing up today, this is viewed as normal behavior as opposed to abnormal and unacceptable behavior. However, none of the aforementioned things have the effect upon our youth that one particular factor has had. This largely influential factor is when children witness domestic violence in their own homes first hand.

Statistics show that "witnessing violence between one's parents or caretakers is the strongest risk factor of transmitting violent behavior from one generation to the next".5 Boys who witness domestic violence are twice as likely to abuse their own partners and children when they become adults.6 What we are seeing is simply transference from one generation to the next. 3.3 million children witness domestic violence each year in the US.7 We are warned over and over again throughout scripture of the power of our influence upon others. We see passages about being the salt of the earth and letting our lights shine before men (Matt. 5:13-16). Paul warned that "evil communication corrupts good manners" (1 Cor. 15:33). Our children are especially impacted by the way we act. Fathers are commanded to bring up their children in the "nurture and admonition of the Lord" (Eph. 6:4). However, when fathers are seen abusing their wives, the example is impressed upon the child that they should do as their father has done. Even if the father tells his children not to act as he acts, the damage is done by what the child has seen.

It is not just that the children see the violence firsthand; many of them experience it as well. Thirty to sixty percent of perpetrators of intimate partner violence also abuse children in the household.8 It is no wonder domestic violence is a problem that continues to grow in our society. Those children who are victims of such abuse grow up thinking in their minds that abuse is the norm. The lives of children are molded and shaped by their parents more than by anyone else. How many times have we seen ourselves become our parents in our adult years? Perhaps it is in our parenting styles, our mannerisms, or what we say. There is no greater influence on the life of an individual than that of their parents. If children continue to see domestic violence in the home or on television, they will simply continue to repeat what they learn.

CAUSES OF DOMESTIC VIOLENCE

What exactly causes a person to become abusive toward a spouse, child, or someone else in the home? There are several different things that could contribute to this. We have already alluded to a few causes. For example, one such cause as we have mentioned is that violence has become a learned behavior. Someone may be an abuser because that is what they learned in their home growing up. Another cause is simply pride or power. Those who abuse generally do so because they are seeking power and control over the other individual. Listen to the following statement that lists some factors in this need for power and control:

Abusers' efforts to dominate their partners have been attributed to low self-esteem or feelings of inadequacy, unresolved childhood conflicts, the stress of poverty, hostility and resentment toward women (misogyny), hostility and resentment toward men (misandry), personality disorders, genetic tendencies and sociocultural influences, among other possible causative factors. Most authorities seem to agree that abusive personalities result from a combination of several factors, to varying degrees.9

There may be psychological issues that are involved such as mental disorders, personality disorders, psychopathy, jealousy, or other things. Even stress can be a factor leading to someone being abusive at home. Keep in mind it is not usually one factor, but several that contribute to domestic violence.

WHAT IS THE BIG DEAL?

Understanding the problem is certainly a huge step in the right direction. However, we still must solve the problem at hand. Remember, it is not just about the physical abuse, but the verbal and emotional abuse as well. In fact, verbal and emotional abuse may be more prevalent among Christians than physical abuse. Some may think just because they do not physically assault another, they are doing no wrong. There needs to be education on what exactly is considered abuse and domestic violence. This all points back to understanding the problem. Once we understand and recognize what abuse and domestic violence is, we must also come to an understanding that it is wrong. Only then can we begin to truly repent and move forward for the better.

So then, what does the Bible say about how we should treat others? Does it address the problem of domestic violence and abuse? If you are looking for a passage that says, "Thou shalt not abuse thy spouse in word or in deed" or "Thou shalt not be abusive towards thy kids," you may be hard pressed to find it. However, what you will find are many verses that deal with the correct way to treat others, including our families. So let's examine those.

Let's begin with the simple idea of love. It permeates throughout God's Word. God loved us so much that He sent His only Son to die so we could spend an eternity with Him in heaven (Jn. 3:16). How many of us would be willing to sacrifice one of our children for a group of people who did not deserve it? Any person who claims to know God is a person that should love. 1 John 4:8 says, "He that loveth not knoweth not God; for God is love." Anyone who is a child of God understands this idea. John goes a little further in verse 11 when he writes, "Beloved, if God so loved us, we ought also to love one another." This idea matches perfectly with what Christ said in Matthew 22:39 when He gave the commandment that is second only to loving God. He said, "And the second is like unto it, Thou shalt love thy neighbour as thyself.'" We understand that the idea of loving our neighbor means loving any and everyone we come in contact with. We see this when Jesus was asked by a lawyer about who was considered our neighbor in Luke 10:29-37. The Bible goes beyond just telling us to love our neighbors. Jesus even commanded us to love our enemies (Matt. 5:43-47). The Bible also commands that husbands are to love their wives. This is not just some common love, as many in the world may think today. Paul wrote in Ephesians 5:25 that husbands should love their wives "even as Christ also loved the church, and gave himself for it". He went on in verse 28-29 to say, "So ought men to love their wives as their own bodies. He that loveth his wife loveth himself. For no man ever yet hated his own flesh; but nourisheth and cherisheth it, even as the Lord the church". How should a husband treat his wife? Not as some object to be owned and controlled, but rather as one who he would nourish, cherish, and die for. Paul repeats some of the same sentiments in Colossians 3:19 where he says, "Husbands, love your wives, and be not bitter against them." Sounds like a command that excludes abuse in the home, doesn't it? Another verse that stands out about the husband wife relationship is found in 1 Peter 3:7. It reads, "Likewise, ye husbands, dwell with them according to knowledge, giving honour unto the wife…" We also find passages that teach this kind of love and treatment toward children. Colossians 3:21 reads, "Fathers, provoke not your children to anger, lest they be discouraged." What would discourage a child more than being physically or verbally abused by his father? Titus 2:4 commands that older women should "teach the young women to be sober, to love their husbands, to love their children". There should be no question concerning the fact we are taught to love in the Bible.

Then, how exactly does love behave and manifest itself? How exactly do we define love? What if someone attempted to explain their abuse by saying they are only doing it out of love? Consider with me the definition of love found in 1 Corinthians 13. If you recall, verse 4 begins by telling us love is both patient and kind. An abuser would probably not be characterized as someone who is patient and kind. Domestic violence and abuse are not loving actions and are sinful in the sight of God. The same passage of scripture tells us love does not envy. That word "envy" means to be jealous over. We have already pointed out jealousy is one of the contributing factors to domestic violence. If we love as the Bible commands, we will not have a jealousy that will cause us to be abusive. Love is also defined as not being puffed up or arrogant. Abusers are normally dealing with a pride or arrogance issue. Verse 5 goes on to further prove that true, Biblical love has no place in domestic violence. It says, "Doth not behave itself unseemly, seeketh not her own, is not easily provoked, thinketh no evil". Certainly we see these traits continue to reinforce positive behavior toward one another.

Again, let us remember this description of love is not just in regard to our actions, but to our words as well. Someone once said, "Sticks and stones may break my bones, but words will never hurt me". That statement could not be further from the truth. Our words can, and do, hurt. The verbal abuse that takes place in the home can do so much damage. James said the tongue is very difficult to control and is full of deadly poison (3:8). The Bible tells us how we ought to speak to each other as well. Paul wrote "Let your speech be alway with grace, seasoned with salt" (Col. 4:6). He wrote again similarly, "Let no corrupt communication proceed out of your mouth, but that which is good to the use of edifying, that it may minister grace unto the hearers" (Eph. 4:29). Just a few verses later in verse 32 Paul said, "And be ye kind one to another, tenderhearted…" Certainly God's Word continues to be as plain and clear as possible when it comes to telling us how we ought to treat one another. Being abusive toward another person, whether it be physically, verbally, sexually, emotionally, or financially, is contrary to God's will and His word and is sin. Paul listed some sins in Romans 1:28-32 (NKJV) that are "worthy of death". Some of those include "maliciousness…strife…evil-mindedness…violent, proud…unloving, unforgiving, unmerciful". More evidence could be given, but what has been mentioned should be sufficient for a child of God trying to be pleasing to the Lord.

WHAT IS THE SOLUTION?

How do we go about putting an end to this horrible problem we face in our country and in the world? There are several things we can do to try and help things get better. One is to educate Christians everywhere. We need to help them understand what domestic violence is and that it affects so many people, even those within the church. We need to diligently teach our kids how they should treat others, especially their future mate and children. By teaching them what it means to love and treat others with respect and kindness, we are laying a foundation for the future. Proverbs 22:6 says, “Train up a child in the way he should go: and when he is old, he will not depart from it.” We have a responsibility to teach our kids how to treat others.

Also by educating people, it may help them to identify or open their eyes to the possibility of domestic violence going on around them. We need to give those who are being abused the courage to come forward and seek help for themselves, and for the abuser. Remember as long as the abuse goes unpunished, people will continue in their same pattern of behavior. There are places where men and women who feel threatened can go in secret and be protected from their abusers. As for the Lord’s church, we must have the courage to stand up against those who commit such a crime and speak out against this sin!

What about those who admit to having a problem with domestic violence and abuse? What if someone comes forward or confides in us they are an abuser? We have the responsibility of taking the appropriate action to ensure that it ceases. We should not just take the abuser’s word for it; we need to continually check on the spouse or children involved and speak with them away from the abuser where they will have more courage to speak openly. This is not to serve as a punishment to the one who confesses his or her struggle with abuse, but rather to help keep them from the temptation of abusing again. We need to realize this is a heart issue, according to what Jesus taught (Matt. 12:34-36; 15:18-20). Therefore we need to deal with the person’s heart and fix the issue from the foundation up. Many who come forward and confess this sin will also require some type of counseling along with anger or emotional management classes. Sometimes these courses can last up to a year and will likely be mandatory for one who goes before a judge on a domestic violence count.

We also need to spend much time in prayer over this issue. We need to pray for ourselves, that we are not lifted up by our pride to commit this type of abuse. We should also pray for our fellow men and women, especially those within the body of Christ. Paul commanded us to pray without ceasing (1 Thess. 5:17) and these prayers should include this petition. Jesus prayed that we be led not into temptation but delivered from the evil one (Matt. 6:13). That would certainly be appropriate in this case. Also remember we are told to cast our cares upon God because He cares for us (1 Pet. 5:7). "The effectual fervent prayer of a righteous man availeth much" (Js. 5:16).

CONCLUSION

The reason we call something an "elephant in the room" is not just because it is a large issue, but rather because it generally goes ignored. We can no longer ignore the issue of domestic violence in the church. It is a sin that affects not just those outside the walls of our buildings, but those who gather inside those same walls. We have just as much of a responsibility to speak out against this social issue as we do the other pressing issues of our day. If we do nothing, then Satan will continue his reign in the lives of those who choose to abuse others. There are many who are enslaved to this sin that need to be set free by the knowledge and direction of Jesus Christ and His word (Jn. 8:32). May God help us to have the courage to combat this evil in our society today!

STUDY QUESTIONS

1. What percentage of women in this country is affected by domestic violence?

2. Besides physical abuse, what other types of abuse does domestic violence consist of?

3. What is one who abuses looking to gain or maintain over the person they are abusing?

4. What are some reasons why domestic violence cases are increasing in our country?

5. What did Solomon say would happen when a sentence against an evil work is not executed speedily according to Ecclesiastes 8:11?

6. What do statistics show is the strongest risk factor of transmitting violent behavior from one generation to the next?

7. What are some of the characteristics of love that are taught in I Corinthians 13 and how do they apply to our relationships in the home?

8. What does the Bible teach us about the words we use towards others?

9. What are the benefits of educating others on this issue?

10. Does it help or hinder when we keep a check on those who have admitted to abusing others in the past?

WORKS CITED

1. Tjaden, Patricia & Thoennes, Nancy. National Institute of Justice and the Centers of Disease Control and Prevention, "Extent, Nature and Consequences of Intimate Partner Violence: Findings from the National Violence Against Women Survey," (2000).

2. National Coalition Against Domestic Violence, http://www.ncadv.org/files/DomesticViolenceFactSheet(National).pdf , NCADV Public Policy Office, 1633 Q St NW #210, Washington, DC 20009.

3. "About Domestic Violence". Office of Violence Against Women. Via Wikipedia entry on Domestic Violence at http://en.wikipedia.org/wiki/ Domestic_violence

4. Tjaden, Patricia & Thoennes, Nancy. National Institute of Justice and the Centers of Disease Control and Prevention, "Extent, Nature and Consequences of Intimate Partner Violence: Findings from the National Violence Against Women Survey," (2000).

5. National Coalition Against Domestic Violence, http://www.ncadv.org/files/DomesticViolenceFactSheet(National).pdf , NCADV Public Policy Office, 1633 Q St NW #210, Washington, DC 20009.

6. Strauss, Gelles, and Smith, "Physical Violence in American Families: Risk Factors and Adaptations to Violence" in 8,145 Families. Transaction Publishers (1990).

7. "Effects On Children". Via Wikipedia entry on Domestic Violence at http://en.wikipedia.org/wiki/Domestic_violence

8. Edelson, J.L. (1999). "The Overlap Between Child Maltreatment and Woman Battering." Violence Against Women. 5:134-154.

9. "Cause: Social Theories: Power and Control". Via Wikipedia entry on Domestic Violence at http://en.wikipedia.org/wiki/Domestic_violence

HOMOSEXUALITY

Johnie Scaggs, Jr.

INTRODUCTION

The moral fiber of our country is rapidly declining. For many years we have seen the downward spiral of our nation as it relates to unborn babies, domestic violence, alcohol and others drugs, pornography, an increase in divorce, dishonesty and lying. Recently, we have seen the increase in the area of the homosexual agenda. As Christians, we must fight against all immoral things, including homosexuality. It is difficult to understand how a "Christian" can try to justify the lifestyle of the homosexual, but many do. Many will try to justify the homosexual lifestyle by saying "they cannot help themselves; they were born this way." When quoting the Bible as it relates to the homosexual, some will say, "the Bible is outdated and not with the modern times." Others will state that "homosexuality is a disease." We hope to answer the question to these things and others as we study this important topic.

THE HOMOSEXAUL AGENDA

Have you ever asked yourself; just what is the agenda of the homosexual movement? The answer to this question is an "eye-opener." In the Gay Community News, February 15, 1987, Michael Swift was invited to write the guest editorial and here is what he wrote:

> We shall sodomize your sons, we shall seduce them in your schools, in your dormitories, in your gymnasiums, in your locker rooms, in your youth

> groups, your sons shall become our minions and do our bidding. They will come to crave and adore us. All laws banning homosexual activity will be revoked. Instead, legislation shall be passed which engenders love between men. Our writers and artists will make love between men fashionable.... We shall raise vast, private armies...to defeat you. The family unit....will be abolished. Perfect boys will be conceived and grown in the genetic laboratory...All churches who condemn us will be closed. Our only gods are handsome young men. All males who insist on remaining stupidly heterosexual will be tried in homosexual courts of justice and will become invisible men. Tremble, hetero swine, when we appear before you without our masks.

It is later than we think, for this is what they are in the process of doing at this present time. Focus on the Family provides additional quotes from "After the Ball," outlining key points of the homosexual agenda. This is the six-point plan they have set forth as to how they could transform the beliefs of ordinary Americans with regard to homosexual behavior in a decade-long time frame:

1. "Talk about gays and gayness as loudly and as often as possible." (They use late night air waves and special channels, as well as their right to peacefully assemble to do so.)
2. "Portray gays as victims, not as aggressive challengers."
3. "Give homosexual protectors a just cause."
4. "Make gays look good."
5. "Make the victimizers look bad."
6. "Get funds from corporate America."

Does all this sound familiar? This is what we are seeing today throughout our society. Those who are promoting the homosexual agenda are militant in their actions. It is their objective to destroy your children by subverting everything they have been taught at home and church that is morally right.

In a 1992 report by John Leo in U.S. News and World Report, he notes some books which were part of New York City's public school curriculum.

The first-grade book, "Children of the Rainbow", stated on page 145, which says teachers must "be aware of varied family structures, including...gay or lesbian parents," and "children must be taught to acknowledge the positive aspects of each type of household." Another children's book is Heather Has Two Mommies, which is about a lesbian couple having a child through artificial insemination. Another book, Gloria Goes to Gay Pride, states, "Some women love women, some men love men, some women and men love each other. That's why we march in the parade, so everyone can have a choice."

Since 1992, many other books have been written which promote the lifestyle of the homosexual and are being taught in many schools.

Leo commented,

> A line is being crossed here; in fact, a brand new ethic is descending upon the city's public school system. The traditional civic virtue of tolerance (if gays want to live together, it's their own business) has been replaced with a new ethic requiring approval and endorsement (if gays want to live together, we must 'acknowledge the positive aspects' of their way of life).

The evidence is overwhelming; their diabolical plan is to destroy all we have taught our children and replace it with their moral standard which is, there are no morals and everyone can do whatever their heart desire. In the process of doing this, they will remove God from the minds of our children. It is time to speak out and say "enough is enough."

A LIFESTYLE CHOICE OR NOT?

Many believe the homosexual cannot help himself because he was born to be a homosexual. This view has been promoted for many years without the slightest bit of evidence. We should note as one reads what others have written on this matter the author(s) of this view. Some of these men who have studied in this area are homosexuals, and thus their studies will be misleading because they will have a strong motivation to justify the lifestyle of the homosexual.

Masters and Johnson (in their book, Human Sexuality, JS) leading sex researchers in America, state, "The genetic theory of homosexuality has been generally discarded today… No serious scientist suggests that a simple cause-effect relationship applies."

Richard Cohen, M.A. (who is a reformed homosexual) in his book Coming Out Straight defines homosexuality by stating:

> (1) Homosexuality is a symptom. (2) Homosexuality is an emotionally based condition. (3) Homosexuality is a Same-Sex Attachment Disorder. He then gives a list of 10 factors which often causes one to become a homosexual.
>
> **Major Causes of Same-Sex Attractions**
>
> There is a constellation of contributing variables that may lead an individual to experience same-sex attractions. The sum is greater than the parts. It is the combination of the following causes that may lead to

> homosexual ideation in either the male or female. A single factor does not cause a Same-Sex Attachment Disorder. It is the confounding of several variables that will lead an individual to experience same-sex attractions. The ten variables are: 1) Heredity, 2) Temperament, 3) Hetero-Emotional Wounds, 4) Homo-Emotional Wounds, 5) Sibling Wounds/Family Dynamics, 6) Body-Image Wounds, 7) Sexual Abuse, 8) Social or Peer Wounds, 9) Cultural Wounds, and 10) Other Factors….There are also differences between male and female homosexuality. In my years of practice, I have observed that many homosexual females are attracted to men, but the majority of homosexual males have no attraction to women. Many homosexual females have been so hurt by men that they turn to women for their affectional needs. However, their attraction to men may still exist. Therefore, the psychology behind male and female homosexuality is different.

The word, "Heredity" is not to be mistaken as referring to genetics, but rather it refers to "Inherited wounds, unresolved family issues, misperceptions, mental filters, predilection for rejection." Every child is born into a family with different problems and often these problems help in the development of the homosexual. We must be very careful as to the treatment of children from within the family and from those people who are not in the family. Sometimes children are treated so badly by family members and their peers that it leaves deep emotional wounds. We should never label children as being weird, or say things like, "you are a homo," or "you look gay, etc." These words and others like them can cause deep wounds that often will be played out in their adult life.

Do not misunderstand my motive in writing these things. I am not attempting to justify the homosexual or make excuses for their actions. We do, however, need to understand the factors involved in their development if we are going to be able to help them. We must remember--they have a soul and they need to hear the truth. Like others who are caught up in sin, they can and must repent, thus changing from walking in the world and beginning to walk with the Lord. Homosexual is a choice; it is not a genetic condition and as such all men must choose what they will do. We should heed to the words of Joshua "And if it seem evil unto you to serve the LORD, choose you this day whom ye will serve; whether the gods which your fathers served that were on the other side of the flood, or the gods of the Amorites, in whose land ye dwell: but as for me and my house, we will serve the LORD" (Josh. 24:15). All mankind must choose either to serve the god of this world or the God of heaven.

If the homosexual is what he is due to genetics, then he could not change, but there are thousands of both men and women who have changed and no longer live the lifestyle of the homosexual. Over several years Psychotherapist Richard Cohen has led numerous men and women out of this lifestyle and they are now living heterosexual lives. Even the Bible teaches this fact.

Do you not know that the unrighteous will not inherit the kingdom of God? Do not be deceived. Neither fornicators, nor idolaters, nor adulterers, nor homosexuals, nor sodomites, nor thieves, nor covetous, nor drunkards, nor revilers, nor extortioners will inherit the kingdom of God. And such were some of you. But you were washed, but you were sanctified, but you were justified in the name of the Lord Jesus and by the Spirit of our God (1 Cor. 6:9-11) NKJV

What did they do? They came out of the sins they were practicing and became Christians. Some of these who did this were homosexuals.

Masters and Johnson stated "a 71.6% success rate in helping men to discontinue their homosexual life-style." If the homosexual problem is a genetic problem, then why and how could Masters and Johnson have such a high rate of success?

HOW DOES GOD VIEW THE SIN OF THE HOMOSEXUAL?

There is an increasing amount of people who claim that homosexuality is really not condemned by God. In this they are sadly mistaken. God has much to say about the homosexual and the life he has chosen to live. God created all things according to the Genesis account of creation. On the sixth day Moses stated, "So God created man in his own image, in the image of God created he him; male and female created he them" (Gen. 1:27). Notice, God "created he him; male and female." According to verses twenty-four and twenty-five, all things are to be after their kind. It is a biological fact all living creatures produce their own kind. How can the homosexual produce their own kind? They cannot; God did not create male and male or female and female, but rather male and female. The homosexual is the only one of its kind that must recruit from another kind in order to continue to produce their own kind. The very fact that God ordained marriage between a man and a woman teaches us that God is not pleased with any other kind of relationship. Those today that are pushing the view that it is okay for homosexuals to marry are doing so without any Biblical support.

God does not endorse homosexual relationships. Nowhere in the Bible can one find even a hint that God endorses homosexuals. He clearly shows His disdain for their sin. The destruction of Sodom and Gomorrah should show people God will not tolerate sin. The Bible is clear that it was because of the sin of homosexuality that God destroyed these two cities and other cities around them (Gen. 19:4-11) Jude writes, "And the angels who did not keep their proper domain, but left their own abode, He has reserved in everlasting chains under darkness for the judgment of the great day; as Sodom and Gomorrah, and the cities around them in a similar manner to these, having given themselves over to sexual immorality and gone after strange flesh, are set forth as an example, suffering the vengeance of eternal fire" (Jude 6-7—NKJV). God hated homosexuality so much that He placed the penalty of death on those who engaged in it. "If a man lies with a male as he lies with a woman, both of them have committed an abomination. They shall surely be put to death. Their blood shall be upon them" (Lev. 20:13-14 —NKJV). If a man or a woman would lie with a beast, both the person and the beast would be put to death (Lev. 20:15-16).

The New Testament likewise condemns this sexual perversion. Paul writes,

> For this reason God gave them up to vile passions. For even their women exchanged the natural use for what is against nature. Likewise also the men, leaving the natural use of the woman, burned in their lust for one another, men with men committing what is shameful, and receiving in themselves the penalty of their error which was due. And even as they did not like to retain God in their knowledge, God gave them over to a debased mind, to do those things which are not fitting; being filled with all unrighteousness, sexual immorality, wickedness, covetousness, maliciousness; full of envy, murder, strife, deceit, evil-mindedness; they are whisperers, backbiters, haters of God, violent, proud, boasters, inventors of evil things, disobedient to parents, undiscerning, untrustworthy, unloving, unforgiving, unmerciful; who, knowing the righteous judgment of God, that those who practice such things are deserving of death, not only do the same but also approve of those who practice them (Rom. 1:26-32).

Paul teaches us that those who practice such things as homosexuality are doing that which is "contrary to sound doctrine" (1 Tim. 1:10).

During the personal minister of our Lord, He even taught against the practice of homosexuality. Wayne Jackson on this point wrote;

> Some argue that Jesus Christ never censured homosexuality, and that He surely would have, had such been morally reprehensible. When the Lord condemned fornication (Mark 7:21-23), He condemned all forms of sexual perversion, including homosexuality (Dictionary of New Testament Theology, pages 497-501). Further, the Son of God taught that a divinely sanctioned marital relationship is between a male and a female (Matthew 19:4-6). There is not a solitary reference in the entire Bible which would suggest that God endorses homosexual activity or relationship.

It is clear from both the Old Testament and the New Testament, God does not endorse homosexuality but rather He condemns such and so must we.

WHAT IS OUR RESPONSIBILITY TOWARD THE HOMOSEXUAL?

We must at all times preach the truth as the Word of God directs us on any issue; this includes homosexuality. We are to love the person while hating the sin. We are to love even our enemies, "You have heard that it was said, 'You shall love your neighbor and hate your enemy.' But I say to you, love your enemies, bless those who curse you, do good to those who hate you, and pray for those who spitefully use you and persecute you" (Matt. 5:43-44—NKJV). Remember, Jesus died for all mankind (John 3:16). It is wrong to make fun of them and call them names. We are to approach them in the spirit of humility with the understanding that they have a soul which needs to be saved. Can they change? Absolutely, they can change and they must if they are going to please the Lord.

CONCLUSION

We live in very trying times. We are being told that if we do not accept those who practice homosexuality that we are homophobic and we are showing our ignorance by not getting with the 21st century. We should, however, realize God's Word does not change for anyone or for any time. All mankind is subject to the same law of God, and they must comply if they are to have salvation.

Let us pray for those who are caught up in sin, and pray that we do not do likewise. May God be glorified in all we do.

STUDY QUESTIONS

1. What are some of the things the Homosexual will say to justify their actions?
2. Michael Swift wrote in what paper about the agenda of the homosexual movement?
3. Focus on the Family gave how many points on the homosexual agenda?
4. It is the objective of the homosexual movement to destroy our children?
5. What are some of the names of books being put into school systems?
6. Richard Cohen defines homosexuality by three things, what are they?
7. Is homosexuality a choice?
8. What does 1 Cor. 6:9-11say about homosexuals?
9. What is our responsibility toward the homosexual?
10. What scripture would you use to show the sin of homosexuality?

WORKS CITED

Yinger, Gary (Seduction to Destruction:) The Homosexual Agenda, http://www.jesus-is-savior.com/Evils%20in%20 America/Sodomy /homosexual_agenda.htm

Focus on the Family http://conservapedia.com/Homosexual_Agenda

Cohen, Richard MA Coming Out Straight Oakhill Press, Winchester, Virginia. 1999

Jackson, Wayne Homosexuality: A Growing Problem Christian Courier, Dec., 1992

GAMBLING

Riley Nelson

INTRODUCTION

Gambling is an activity that is growing more popular with each passing year. Most states have established "lotteries" which bring in millions of dollars. In most convenience stores one must wait in line several minutes while someone plays their numbers and buys more tickets. Thousands of tickets are bought by those, who for the hope of instant riches, squander their food and rent money. Families have been destroyed by this sinful activity. Christians must have a clear understanding of the issue of gambling. Like many other words, the word "gambling" can be used in various ways. For instance one might say that flying on an airplane is "gambling with one's life," while others believe that gambling is any activity involving chance. However, this idea is too general for a proper understanding of the word:

The World Book Encyclopedia of 1958 described gambling in this manner:

> Gambling means staking something of value in a game of chance. True games of chance require no skill on the part of the player. Their outcome depends entirely on luck. People gamble because they hope to win something for nothing. But one can more easily lose, and the loss may involve money which was earned by hard effort and which may be difficult to replace. A serious loss often causes hardship. Hence it is not considered desirable or wise for anyone to gamble.

Similarly, Jim Waldron on his chapter in the book, "Is There a Universal Code of Ethics" quoted Edward C. Devereux, saying:

> Gambling is betting on the outcome of a future event. A gambler usually bets money or something else of value as a stake on the outcome he predicts. When the outcome is settled, the winner collects the loser's stakes. People gamble most often on games of chance, such as dice or card games. But they also gamble on games of skill, horse racing and other sports, elections, and almost any event with and unpredictable outcome.

Additionally, in a sermon entitled "How Much Risk is Gambling?" Stafford North stated that "Gambling is the act of risking what is yours to get what belongs to another and nothing is given in return". In contrast, gambling is not simply activities involving chance. Farmers plant crops, which involves risks, but that is not gambling. The farmer does not leave everything to chance; he does all he can to insure his crops are fruitful. Some believe buying insurance is gambling. However, the person buying an insurance policy pays the insurance company to avoid the consequences of the risks that already exist. Gambling involves taking a risk or chance specifically for some stake, be it money or material good.

THE PROBLEM

Gambling is a vice that many, even some members of the Lord's church, see as harmless entertainment. Some consider gambling to be a "gray" area, and that God has not described gambling as good or bad. Those who believe this have not taken the time to consider the various aspects of gambling, and as Christians, they have neglected the most important perspective of consideration, the Biblical perspective. The apostle Paul wrote, "And be not conformed to this world: but be ye transformed by the renewing of your mind, that ye may prove what is that good, and acceptable, and perfect, will of God" (Rom. 12:2). In the past, those who gambled were seen as worldly and ungodly people. Recently, this idea has changed as the government has used gambling as a way to raise money for schools, roads and other items.

Another difficulty with gambling exists, because many people gauge gambling's acceptability by the circumstances involved in the game. In the context of casinos or behind closed doors, hidden from polite society, games such as poker or blackjack are opposed. There are those who oppose these activities but yet they have no compunction to play bingo for money or buy raffle tickets for a good cause, or "flipping" a coin to see who buys a soft drink. Many a young man has suffered the hand of discipline from his mother for "pitching" pennies, while she clutched her raffle ticket in the other hand.

Gambling is also associated with a rise in crime rates in areas where casinos exist. In the sixties and seventies, organized crime became involved with gambling casinos and hotels in Las Vegas. In the state of Nevada, because of lax regulations members of organized crime, syndicates were able to own and operate gambling establishments. Because of this influence, casino gambling has become one of the most regulated businesses in America. This regulation helped to remove the organized crime syndicates from most casinos. Safeguards have been put into place to guard against organized crime gaining a foothold on the industry again. Despite the regulations that have been put in place gambling, it is still associated with crime, due mainly to the amount of cash that is involved.

Since the government's involvement in regulating gambling has come about, the industry has worked to change its image. Now instead of courting just gamblers, the casinos offer "family attractions". They have built theme-park hotels with "family friendly" attractions, offering free meals and cheap accommodations. The idea is to attract a larger base of people to the area with hopes that they will gamble while they are there. Las Vegas runs a television ad stating, "Whatever happens in Vegas stays in Vegas" This is another snare to draw in the crowds.

Gambling has spread to nearly every state through state run "lotteries". Millions of dollars are spent trying to win the "big one". Gambling, especially the lottery, is harming thousands of people without their realization. In an article entitled "The Facts About the Lottery" by the Sooner Alcohol Narcotics Education group, the following information is given.

A California study revealed that 40% of lottery players are unemployed. (*ALCAP) In Maryland, the poorest 1/3 of the population buys 60% of the daily numbers tickets. (ALCAP) In Georgia, those who make less than $25,000 a year spend three times as much on lottery tickets than those who make $75,000 or more per year (*AFA) On the national average, lottery gamblers with household incomes under $10,000 dollars bet nearly 3 times as much on the lottery as those with incomes over $50,000. (*ERLC) A 1988 New Jersey study found that among lottery players with income of less than $10,000 per year, the average percentage of income spent on lottery tickets was almost 21%. (ERLC) In Massachusetts, individuals in the poorer cities of Worcester and Chelsea spent an average of $336 and $445, respectively, on lottery tickets in the early 1990s. Those in wealthier towns such as Weston and Amherst spent an average of $30 and $42, respectively. (AFA) A University of Texas study found that players with a high school diploma or less spent more than $250 a year on the lottery. (AFA)

In Michigan, a 1994 study in Detroit found that people with less than a high school diploma spend over five times more than those with a college degree spend. (AFA) In New Mexico, in 1996, three of its poorest counties ranked among the top-10 best-selling counties in lottery ticket sales. (AFA) A 1996 Virginia Lottery study found that 13% of those who purchased tickets said playing the lottery reduced the money they would normally spend on household expenses. (AFA) Economics Professor and lottery expert, Dr. Robert Goodman, says that after 3 to 5 years, many people stop playing the lottery because they can no longer afford it. ("The Luck Business," by Dr. Robert Goodman)

The lottery exploits people of every age; older Americans are the fastest growing group of problem gamblers. The lure of being the one to win the jackpot is too much for some people. They never stop to consider the odds until they have wasted hundreds of dollars and some have spent their life savings trying to win. Consider these statistics, which give the odds of winning the lottery.

The odds of winning the lottery are… 1 chance in 54 million (ERLC) The chance of winning a jackpot like the record-setting Powerball lottery that occurred in May, 1998 is 1 in 80 million! Compare this to your chances of experiencing some other incidents in life. You have…

a 1 in 3 million chance of freezing to death

a 1 in 2 million chance of being struck by lightning

a 1 in 1 million chance of dying in the bath tub

1 chance in 700,000 of being killed by a dog

1 chance in 86,000 of dying from poisoning (Baton Rouge Advocate)

A lottery ticket buyer is… 5 times more likely to be eaten by a shark 6,000 times more likely to be hit by a car 500,000 times more likely to die in an airliner crash (Seducing America: Is Gambling a Good Bet? By Rex M. Rogers)

Gambling is devastating to families and to the very sanity of individuals. This "harmless" pastime has caused business men to loss their businesses, and husbands and wives to spend money intended to pay for food and housing to pay their gambling debts.

Studies have shown that lower income families spend more on lotteries than other income levels. Researchers at Duke University conducted a study for the National Gambling Impact Study Commission. Their findings reveal:

> The lottery participation rate generally increases with income, although it falls for people with incomes higher than $100,000; the highest rate of play is for those with incomes between $50,000 and $100,000.

By contrast, the annual amount spent, or per capita play, by gamblers is actually highest for lower-income households ($597 per year), exceeding any other income category, and more than double the amount for the highest earners ($289 per year, on average).

Since many households have more than one adult, and since higher-income households have more adults per household than lower-income households, the study also examines per household spending:

Even after the adjustment, households earning just $10,000 spend twice the amount on gambling as households earning $90,000.

Put another way, the lowest-earning households spend about 10.8 percent of income on gambling, versus 0.7 percent of income for the highest earners. Clearly, lottery expenditures are regressive: Lower earners not only spend larger percentages of their incomes gambling but also spend larger real dollar amounts. As a result, lottery taxes are also regressive, since the implicit lottery tax is incurred as a percent of total purchases, and lower earners pay a greater share of their income in lottery taxes.

Another problem is gambling is an addictive vice that can overcome a person. Most gamblers do not start out to be "compulsive" gamblers; it just seems to happen. There are said to be four characteristics of compulsive gamblers. 1) Dependence--they feel a need to gamble much like an alcoholic needs a drink. 2) Loss of control--the gambler bets when he had no intention of betting or bets more than he intended. 3) Progression--where wagers get larger, the odds become heavier and losses become larger. 4) Debt-ridden--the gambler will beg, borrow, or steal in order to be able to gamble. This is a dangerous, sinful activity.

WHAT DOES THE BIBLE SAY ABOUT GAMBLING?

Christians who seek to justify gambling sometimes will argue that the Bible does not specifically mention the word "gamble." This argument reveals one's need of more Bible study. Garland Elkins and Robert R. Taylor Jr. made the following observation in their tract, Gambling: National Pastime To Prosperity Or Sure Bet To Poverty and Perdition?

Religious proponents, defensive of and favorable to gambling, are always coming up with queries such as, "Where does the Bible condemn gambling? Or where does the Bible say, 'Thou shalt not gamble?'" They will say, "You cannot find the word gamble in the Bible. Neither can we find the explicit words of rape, cocaine, heroin, etc., but participation therein is Biblically condemned for a surety.

Gambling is at odds with the Word of God because it involves risk or taking a chance for money or other such stakes. It is motivated by covetousness which is defined as; 1) inordinately or wrongly desirous of wealth or possessions; 2) greedy, eagerly desirous. Covetousness is sin, which is condemned by God. Paul wrote, "For this ye know, that no whoremonger, nor unclean person, nor covetous man, who is an idolater, hath any inheritance in the kingdom of Christ and of God" (Eph. 5:5). Christians are to put this behavior to death as new creatures in Christ, "Mortify therefore your members which are upon the earth; fornication, uncleanness, inordinate affection, evil concupiscence, and covetousness, which is idolatry: For which things' sake the wrath of God cometh on the children of disobedience:" (Col. 3:5). For this reason, gambling is condemned because of the desire to take something from someone else without a fair exchange for the property.

Still, those who want to gamble argue that they are not covetous; they just do it for fun. If gambling is done just for fun, then take the money out of the picture, and just do it for fun, no gain nor loss. The gambling would stop.

> Gambling also goes against the work ethic taught in God's word. God's plan is for man to work for what he has. "In the sweat of thy face shalt thou eat bread, till thou return unto the ground; for out of it wast thou taken: for dust thou art, and unto dust shalt thou return" (Gen. 3:19). This passage is metaphorical, meaning that man is to work, whether physical, mental or intellectual to make gain. Honest labor and honest wages are what is taught in the Bible. Servants, be obedient to them that are your masters according to the flesh, with fear and trembling, in singleness of your heart, as unto Christ; Not with eye service, as men pleasers; but as the servants of Christ, doing the will of God from the heart; With good will doing service, as to the Lord, and not to men: Knowing that whatsoever good thing any man doeth, the same shall he receive of the Lord, whether he be bond or free. And, ye masters, do the same things unto them, forbearing threatening: knowing that your Master also is in heaven; neither is there respect of persons with him (Eph. 6:5-9).

Paul also wrote, "Let him that stole steal no more: but rather let him labour, working with his hands the thing which is good, that he may have to give to him that needeth" (Eph. 4:28). The gambler has the philosophy of getting without giving, which is condemned by God.

In what has become known as the "golden rule," gambling is condemned. "Therefore all things whatsoever ye would that men should do to you, do ye even so to them: for this is the law and the prophets" (Matt. 7:12). Gamblers do not bet on activities hoping their opponents will take their money; they want the opponent's money. The one who wins the bet takes from another without giving anything in return. This goes against the second greatest command as taught by Jesus, "And the second is like unto it, Thou shalt love thy neighbor as thyself" (Matt. 22:39). Jesus also taught. "A new commandment I give unto you, That ye love one another; as I have loved you, that ye also love one another. By this shall all men know that ye are my disciples, if ye have love one to another" (John 13:34, 35). Is love being shown to one's neighbor, when one attempts to win one's neighbor's money? Some have suggested, "Well they wanted to gamble, they knew the risks". Does this make it right? Christians are to follow God's Word and love others as themselves, to help others, not steal from them, and gambling is a form of stealing. It actually is more akin to the iron rule, than the golden rule.

Another thing to consider is the subject of stewardship. God has blessed man with all the material blessings he has. These blessings must be used in accordance with the Word of God. (2 Cor. 5:10) The gambler might say, "Well I just gamble for entertainment and I set aside money for this and it does not take food from my table, or my contribution to God; it's just for fun". If it is just for fun, what will this person do with the winnings if they win? Will they give them back to the house or to their fellow gamblers? If it is just for entertainment, then why not allow the casino to keep your winnings? The truth of the matter is, they are there to see what they can win and take from another. Poker, blackjack, roulette, and almost any game that can be thought of can be played for fun, without stakes. Why does money have to be involved? Is the gambler a good steward of what God has blessed him with when he places his blessing at risk in order to obtain something for nothing from others?

One must also consider one's example as a Christian. What example does the gambler set before the world, or before fellow Christians? Paul told Timothy to be an "example of the believers" in the way he lived (1 Tim. 4:12). How can one who gambles think he is being a proper example to those around them? While gambling, one is not showing love for God or his fellow man. He is showing the desire to have that which belongs to another to the point of placing his blessings at risk. This does not fit the character of a Christian.

Christians who gamble have tried, and still try, to justify their vice. They have even tried to use the Bible to show gambling was approved in the Bible, citing the casting of lots. Elkins and Taylor dealt with this in their tract:

> There are those who contend that the Bible approved gambling, and they then refer to the assignment of tribal lands (Num. 26:55), office rotation (1 Chron. 24:5), and the selection of the apostle Matthias by lot (Acts 1:26) in the New Testament. However, in each one of these cases it was not a matter of the people's gambling, and by chance arriving at whatever result obtained as in the case of gambling, but rather this was God's way of making His choice known to the people. "The lot is cast into the lap; but the whole disposing thereof is of the LORD" (Prov. 16:33).

WAYS TO AVOID GAMBLING

One of the best ways to avoid gambling is to learn what is, and is not, gambling. Only those who are seeking to be pleasing to God will take the time to do this; others will follow their feelings and do what they like. If a thing is questionable, the best path to follow is not to become involved.

One must remember that the amount involved is not important, and gambling is not defined by the amount of money at stake. When approached to match coins to see who buys the cokes, or when an office pool is started for a sporting event, remember these things are by definition gambling. If a person never participates in these activities, they are less likely to become gamblers.

Also, cautious Christian parents must make sure their children understand gambling is a sin. This will take some study and some teaching on the subject, and perhaps even some sacrifices (by giving up activities to set the proper example before one's children), but their souls are worth the effort.

CONCLUSION

Gambling is becoming more and more popular every year. States using gambling to raise revenue for schools, roads and other projects have caused the way people look at gambling to change. When it was considered illegal, many Christians avoided this vice. However, legal or not, a Christian must look at this activity as well as any other in the light of God's word. Christians are to "Prove all things; hold fast that which is good. Abstain from all appearance of evil" (1 Thess. 5:21, 22). When gambling is looked at in light of the scriptures by an open and honest heart, the Christian will realize this is not an activity in which one may participate.

STUDY QUESTIONS

1. What is the true definition of gambling?
2. What is the difference in a farmer planting a crop and a gambler placing a bet?
3. What is behind the desire to gamble?
4. What attractions are casinos advertising in order to attract crowds?
5. What income level spends more money on gambling (especially the lottery)?
6. What age group seems to be more prone to gamble?
7. What Biblical principles does gambling violate?
8. Why is "gambling for entertainment" a false conception?
9. What is the difference in the casting of lots in the Bible and gambling?
10. Does the amount make a difference as to whether a thing is gambling or not?

ALCOHOL AND THE USE OF TOBACCO AND OTHER DRUGS

Victor M. Eskew

INTRODUCTION

"Alcohol and the Use of Tobacco and Other Drugs," is an extremely timely subject. Approximately 8% of the population of the United States is dependent upon alcohol. 19.3% of the population smoke cigarettes. With regard to illicit drug use, approximately 8.7% of the population has used some form of drugs within the last month.

The church is not immune from alcohol, tobacco, and drugs. Many families have their horror stories of a family member who has been caught in the throes of alcoholism. Many could tell us how a family member died because he/she was addicted to nicotine. Still others could inform us of the hurt that has come to their home because a member of the family was addicted to some type of drug.

In this lesson, we will attempt to do three things. First, we want to briefly discuss some general information about our subject. Second, we will look into the Scriptures and examine some principles and precepts that pertain to our subject. Third, we want to focus specifically upon cigarette smoking. Because of the limited space we have and the enormous subject at hand, we will not be able to address every aspect of this topic. It is this author's hope that you will be given enough information in this lesson to make an informed decision about how you will respond to these things as a Bible believer.

GENERAL INFORMATION

Alcohol, tobacco, and other drugs are intoxicating substances. The word "intoxicated" means "to be affected temporarily with diminished physical and mental control by means of alcoholic liquor, a drug, or other substance." In other words, those who ingest alcohol, tobacco, and other drugs are influenced by these things. Both their bodies and their minds are influenced. DUI means "driving under the influence." Let us point out at the outset of this lesson that we are not speaking of medications that are prescribed by a doctor, that are taken as prescribed, and are monitored by a physician. These things do influence a person when they are taken. The purpose of taking such medications, however, is for health purposes. Even Paul admonished Timothy to "use a little wine for thy stomach's sake and thine often infirmities" (I Tim. 5:23).

Intoxicants are grouped into four different categories: Depressants/Sedatives, Stimulants, Narcotics/Opiates, and Hallucinogens. These categories have been formed due to the ingredients in the drugs and the effects they have upon the users. Depressants are also called "downers." These drugs relieve stress, decrease anxiety, and bring about sleep. Stimulants, on the other hand, are called "uppers." Stimulants tend to relieve malaise and increase alertness. Narcotics are often given to reduce both mental and physical pain. Hallucinogens alter human perception and mood. It should be noted that alcohol falls into the Depressant category. Tobacco falls into the Stimulant category. Caffeine is also a drug and falls into the Stimulant category as well.

There are numerous ways to categorize intoxicating substances. One of the ways they are divided is into legal and illegal substances. Alcohol, tobacco, and medications are legal substances. In other words, it is not against the laws of society to purchase and take them. Illegal drugs involve such things as marijuana, cocaine, and crystal meth. Many are of the opinion that as long as drugs are legal they are acceptable to take. What these individuals fail to take into consideration is a higher law that is, the law of God. Men can make all types of laws that conflict with God's law. History is full of examples of wickedness, evil, and debauchery being legalized by man. When man's law and God's law are in conflict, God's law is the higher order. This lesson is found in Matthew 15:3-9 and Acts 5:27-29. Just because man legalizes something, does not mean the action is approved in the high court of heaven.

BIBLICAL PRINCIPLES TO CONSIDER

When discussing the subject of alcohol, tobacco, and drugs, many want to complicate the issue by raising all kinds of objections. These objections are raised, it seems, in an effort to give approval for the use of intoxicants. This writer believes we should first consider some basic Bible principles, which, if followed, would bring an end to many of the objections. For instance, the Bible is deeply concerned about man's soberness. In Titus 2:1-6, the beloved Paul gives counsel to four groups of people in the church: the aged men, the aged women, the younger women, and the young men. One characteristic is common to them all, soberness. Let us hear the apostle's admonitions:

> But speak thou the things which become sound doctrine: that the aged men be sober, grave, temperate, sound in faith, in charity, in patience. The aged women likewise, that they be in behavior as becometh holiness, not false accusers, not given to much wine, teachers of good things; that they may teach the young women to be sober, to love their husbands, to love their children, to be discreet, chaste, keepers at home, obedient to their own husbands, that the word of God be not blasphemed. Young men likewise exhort to be soberminded.

One of the definitions of sober is "not intoxicated." Intoxicants pollute the mind. Intoxicants alter the mind. Intoxicants do not allow one to think and reason as he should. God wants the mind of man to be clear. He wants man to be able to think rationally. He wants him to be able to make wholesome decisions that are in harmony with His will (Isa. 1:18). This one principle alone should rule out all mind-altering drugs as far as the Christian is concerned. Anything that takes away one's soberness should be considered harmful to the Christian (cf. Prov. 4:23). The moment he allows his mind to be altered, Satan has the ability to influence it for evil.

Some will argue that one drink or one beer or one joint does not affect the mind. This is not true. The moment any chemical enters into the blood stream, the body is affected. Recently this writer saw a billboard that said: "If you have had one drink, you are five times more likely to have an accident." A commercial on the radio states that "buzz driving is drunk driving." Some argue that they have built up a tolerance to alcohol. The terminology they use proves our point. There was a time when one drink did what it now takes three drinks to do. One drink, therefore, did alter their mind and body in the past. That is our point. It still does, but only more slowly. Their host and friend, named alcohol, is deceiving them. The wise writer of Proverbs warned about this. "Wine is a mocker, strong drink is raging: and whosoever is deceived thereby is not wise" (Prov. 20:1).

Another principle taught in the Bible is abstinence. Paul wrote these words to the church in Thessalonica: "Abstain from all appearance of evil" (1 Thess. 5:22). Peter issued a similar admonition in 1 Peter 2:11. "Dearly beloved, I beseech you as strangers and pilgrims, abstain from fleshly lusts, which war against the soul." The word "abstain" means to "hold oneself off from" or "to refrain." Are intoxicants associated with evil? Yes. Are intoxicants a fleshly lust? Yes. Since the answers to these questions are yes, the child of God should refrain from them. Please note that partaking in a limited manner is not abstinence. We understand this in other areas of morality. When young people engage in some sexual activity short of intercourse, we do not think this is abstinence. When a person robs a store of a candy bar instead of robbing a bank, he has not practiced abstinence from theft. When one views a Playboy versus watching a full-length pornographic movie, he has not abstained from porn. Why then do we think we can drink a little and still practice abstinence from alcohol? Abstinence and drinking are opposite actions. The Bible says to abstain. Again, we have found a Bible principle that is easy to understand and one that should settle the mind of the Christian in regard to taking intoxicants.

Another principle in the Bible that conflicts with the taking of intoxicants is the Christian's influence. Jesus exhorts us to be salt and light in the world.

> Ye are the salt of the earth: but if the salt have lost his savour, wherewith shall it be salted? It is thenceforth good for nothing, but to be cast out, and to be trodden under foot of men. Ye are the light of the world. A city that is set on a hill cannot be hid. Neither do men light a candle, and put it under a bushel, but on a candlestick; and it giveth light unto all that are in the house. Let your light so shine before men, that they may see your good works, and glorify you Father which is in heaven (Matt. 5:13-16).

When Paul wrote to Timothy, he commanded him to be an example of the believers in six different areas. "Let no man despise thy youth; but be thou an example of the believers, in word, in conversation, in charity, in spirit, in faith, in purity" (1 Tim. 4:12). Brethren, it is difficult to be salt when you are sitting behind the counter of a bar ordering a beer. It is hard to be the light of the world when some form of illicit drug is coursing through your veins while at a friend's party. It is not easy for a dad to be an example to his children of a non-smoker when he is teaching them with a cigarette hanging from his lips. How does one show the world how to be separate from the world while holding on to the pleasures of the world? The Jews attempted this manner of living in the first century. Their actions only caused the name of God to be blasphemed among the Gentiles.

> Thou therefore which teachest another, teachest thou not thyself? Thou that preachest that a man should not steal, dost thou steal? Thou that sayest a man should not commit adultery, dost thou commit adultery? Thou that abhorest idols, dost thou commit sacrilege? Thou that makest thy boast of the law, through breaking the law dishonorest thou God? For the name of God is blasphemed among the Gentiles through you, as it is written (Rom. 2:21-24).

Another Biblical principle that one should consider when making a decision about taking intoxicants is temperance. This is not a word that is familiar to most. It simply means self-control. Peter includes temperance in his list of the Christian graces that the faithful are to add to their lives.

> And beside this, giving all diligence, add to your faith virtue; and to virtue knowledge; and to knowledge temperance; and to temperance patience; and to patience godliness; and to godliness brotherly kindness; and to brotherly kindness charity (2 Pet. 1:5-7).

The apostle out of due season exhorts us to temperance in 1 Corinthians 9:25. In the context, Paul parallels the Christian life with some of the disciplines of those who participated in the Olympic Games. He writes: "And every man that striveth for the mastery is temperate in all things. Now they do it to obtain a corruptible crown; but we an incorruptible." The Olympic athletes exercised self-control in many areas of life for a long period of time as they trained for the games. They had very strict schedules. Their diets were under constant scrutiny. Exercise and training were routine every day of their life. And, what did they hope to obtain? A corruptible crown. Christians are seeking a crown of much greater value. It will never fade. Thus, we, too, should seek to be temperate in all our ways. Many times intoxicants remove self-control from those who take them. Instead of being in control, those who ingest an intoxicant find that their "drug" becomes their master. They are controlled by it instead of being in control of it. When this happens, one is no longer living a life of temperance. Peter reveals what happens to those who cease adding the Christian graces to his life. "But he that lacketh these things is blind, and cannot see afar off, and hath forgotten that he was purged from his old sins" (2 Pet. 1:9). Few, if any, Christians can practice some semblance of faithfulness while they engage in drinking alcohol and taking drugs. Many are weak at best. Most are not faithful at all. Faithful Christians exert self-control in their lives. They refuse to allow alcohol and drugs to dominate their lives.

Still another Biblical principle to consider when intoxicants become tempting is wisdom. In Ephesians 5:15-16, we read: "See then that ye walk circumspectly, not as fools, but as wise, redeeming the time, because the days are evil." God's children walk wisely. They are individuals who have their eyes open. They are aware of every step that they take. They realize that the wrong step can bring disastrous consequences. When considering intoxicants, they ask: "Is this a wise thing in which to engage?" Their answer is a bold, resounding: "NO!" They are aware of the Biblical description of one who is a drinking man.

1. Arrogance (Hab. 2:5)
2. Bloodshot eyes (Prov. 23:29)
3. Confusion (Prov. 23:23)
4. Forgetfulness (Prov. 31:6-7)
5. Lack of feeling (Prov. 23:31, 35)

6. Poverty (Prov. 23:20-21)

7. Sickness (Isa. 19:14; 28:7-8; Jer. 48:26)

8. Slowing of the thinking processes (Prov. 31:4-5; Isa. 28:7; Hos. 4:11)

9. Staggering (Job 12:25; Isa. 28:7-8; 29:9)

10. Stupor (Jer. 25:27; 51:39)

None of these things seems very wise to the wise Christian. Thus, he abstains. He does not want anything to take him off the strait and narrow (Matt. 7:13-14). He realizes that his time on earth is short. Therefore, he buys up the time for things that are good--not things that are evil, or, even questionable.

The last principle we will consider involves Jesus' example. We are to follow in the footsteps of the Savior. "He that saith he abideth in him ought himself also so to walk, even as he walked" (1 John 2:6). Can anyone really see Jesus purchasing and drinking alcohol? Will anyone admit that he can envision Jesus smoking cigarettes? Will anyone honestly say that he can fathom Jesus taking any illicit drug? Jesus was much too pure and holy to engage in such things. The writer of Hebrews describes Him with these words: "For such a high priest became us, who is holy, harmless, undefiled, separate from sinners, and made higher than the heavens" (Heb. 7:26). Jesus would never lead a person down a path to poverty, destruction, death, and the loss of one's soul. The example of Jesus, if followed, will lead one to heaven. He will never make a detour down a path that would set him on the broad way.

These principles are Biblical in nature. They are clear guidelines for anyone who honestly examines alcohol, tobacco, and drugs. If these principles were followed, no Christian would ever take a drag on a cigarette, a sip from a can of beer, or a toke from a joint of marijuana. The Christian's mind and body would be free from the influence of all intoxicants. He would be sober. His light would always shine brightly. He would be in control, wise, and walking in the way of the Lord. He would diligently abstain from the devil's brew, cancer sticks, and chemicals that are not prescribed and strictly monitored by a doctor.

CIGARETTES

Cigarette smoking is a very difficult subject to broach for a gospel preacher. The reason is because so many Christians engage in the practice. Another reason is because elders will hardly deal with the matter. Also, in some areas of the country, we have Christians who own and operate tobacco farms. Smoking has been taken off of the list of sins and has been put on the list of "hush-hush" matters within the church. In this section, we want to list some of the reasons why a Christian should not smoke. Some of these reasons will definitely put smoking in the "sinful" category.

1. Smoking is a nasty habit. It puts a foul odor in one's mouth. It causes a person's clothes to stink. It turns one's fingers yellow from nicotine stain. It also pollutes our land. Thousands of cigarette butts can be found almost everywhere. I do not smoke and I usually find one or two in or around my lawn and walkways every time I cut the yard.

2. Smoking is an expensive habit. The average pack of cigarettes is somewhere between $4.00 and $5.00. If a person smokes two packs a day, his habit is costing almost $70.00 per week. That is about $300.00 per month. That kind of money could be saved, or, used in the Lord's kingdom. Instead, it is burned up on a daily basis.

3. Smoking is a physically harmful habit. This fact has been known since 1859. It has been emphasized to the

American public since the 1960's. Heart disease, strokes, lung diseases, cancer, reproductive effects, lower bone density, and other ailments have been attributed to smoking. It is involved in one of every five deaths in the United States. This speaker has seen the effects of tobacco personally in the life of his father. My father had emphysema because he smoked. The last two years of his life he was on oxygen. The last year of his life, he was confined to the house. He died in 1997 at the age of 61. Sadly, his death was preventable. Had he not smoked, the chances are very good he would still be with us.

4. Smoking is a materially harmful habit. Smokers have brought harm to many physical things. They have burned holes in their shirts, their car seats, and their carpet at home. Did you know that 56% of all residential fires are attributed to a smoker?

5. Smoking is a habit that may be harmful to others. There have been many studies conducted that show that second-hand smoke can be harmful to others. It can increase their chances of contracting numerous illnesses.

6. Smoking is a deadly habit. In fact, smoking causes more deaths than vehicle accidents, homicides, AIDS, illegal drugs, and fires.

7. Smoking is not an exemplary habit. In our previous section, we studied 1 Timothy 4:12 that exhorts us to be examples to the believers. This writer is not aware of one smoker who is out promoting the use of tobacco. There is not one smoker who is actively going around the country encouraging our youth to smoke. Most smokers are advocates of abstinence when it comes to smoking. They tell young people to never start. This one point alone tells me that smoking is an ungodly habit.

8. Smoking is an enslaving habit. Smokers are not the ones who are in control of their habit. The habit controls them. They MUST have their cigarette. They MUST have their cigarette at the right time. They MUST have their cigarette even if it costs them double what they normally pay for it. If they do not get it, they have symptoms of withdrawal. Their master punishes them if they do not bow at his feet. Just watch a smoker. He can hardly participate in any activity without having to withdraw for a few moments for a smoke. Approximately 70% of all smokers would like to stop, but they have great difficulty in doing so because their body is controlled by the drugs in the cigarettes. Romans 6:12 states: "Let not sin therefore reign in your mortal body, that ye should obey it in the lusts thereof."

9. Smoking is a progressive habit. Smoking starts off with maybe one or two cigarettes a day. It progressively gets worse. Sometimes the habit does not stop with cigarettes. It can lead one to other addictive drugs such as alcohol, marijuana, and cocaine.

10. Smoking is not a Christ-like habit. Most individuals would not say that Jesus would be a smoker if He were on earth today. If Christ would not do it, neither should we. We are to follow in His steps (1 Pet. 2:21).

The concepts that cause smoking to be sinful in the mind of this writer are: 1) Smoking cannot be commended as something for others to do. 2) Smoking enslaves the individual. And, 3) Smoking cannot be considered to be Christ-like. If these things do not put smoking into the realm of sin, why not?

CONCLUSION

The use of alcohol, tobacco, and drugs can be dangerous and deadly. Most would encourage our youth to never get involved in any of these things. Sadly, some will counsel them, saying: "If you do choose to participate, do so with moderation." What is that? Will moderation keep one away from the operating room? Will moderation keep a person from driving under the influence? Will moderation keep one out of jail? Will moderation mean anything when one is diagnosed with cancer or liver problems? Will moderation restore a life that has been addicted to drugs for years and years?

Alcohol, tobacco, and drugs fall into the category of things of the world. As members of the church, we should not have any fellowship with these things. Jesus exhorts us not to be of the world, even as He is not of the world (John 17:16). Paul commands us not to be conformed to the world (Rom. 12:2). John wrote: "Love not the world, neither the things that are in the world. If any man love the world, the love of the Father is not in him" (1 John 2:15). In the Parable of the Sower, Jesus teaches that those who get caught up in the world fail to produce good fruit (Luke 8:14). Brethren, we are the church, the called out ones. Let's live our lives in such a way as to show the world that we are not influenced in any manner by the evils and addictions of this world. If we are going to be addicted to anything, let us be addicted to the ministry of Jesus Christ (1 Cor. 16:15).

STUDY QUESTIONS

1. Many homes have been impacted by drugs and alcohol. Do you have a story from your family?
2. What is the meaning of the word "intoxicated"?
3. What are the four different groups of intoxicants?
4. Does legalizing a substance make if right to take?
5. Why does God command His people to be sober?
6. Does one beer or one joint intoxicate the mind?
7. Why are individuals so opposed to abstinence?
8. Is it possible to socially drink or socially do drugs and be a light to the world as Jesus commanded?
9. Do the points given in this lesson about cigarette smoking convince you that smoking is a sin?
10. Discuss the concept of doing things in moderation.

PORNOGRAPHY

Larry Yarber

INTRODUCTION

The theme for this year's lectures is "MORALS IN AN IMMORAL AGE". Webster defines moral, "moral, mor-al, …of or concerned with the principles of right and wrong in conduct and character; teaching or upholding standards of good behavior; conforming to the rules of right conduct; sexually virtuous; …capable of distinguishing between right and wrong; …ethics; principles and mode of life; behavior as to right or wrong, esp. in relation to sexual matters" - (621). Although neither word, "moral" nor "immoral", appear in the KJV of the Bible, there is no doubt the Bible calls upon Christians to live moral lives and condemns all who practice immorality. Paul penned, "Know ye not that the unrighteous shall not inherit the kingdom of God? Be not deceived, neither fornicators, nor idolaters, nor adulterers, nor effeminate, nor abusers of themselves with mankind, nor thieves, nor covetous, nor drunkards, nor revilers, nor extortioners, shall inherit the kingdom of God" (1 Cor. 6:9-10).

PORNOGRAPHY AND ITS EFFECT UPON SOCIETY

In order to illustrate the negative effect pornography has had on society in general, let's look at some alarming statistics. While the following quotes are not verbatim, they are accurately reported as found on www.familysafemediacom/pornography_statistics.html. "Average age of first internet exposure to pornography - 11 years. Largest consumer of internet pornography - 35 to 49 years. Promise Keeper men who viewed pornography in the last week - 53%. US pornography revenue exceeds the combined revenues of ABC, CBS, and NBC. The pornography industry is larger than the revenues of the top technology companies combined: Microsoft, Google, Amazon, eBay, Yahoo!, Apple, Netflix, and Earthlink. Pornographic web pages by country - US 89%. Top pornography banning countries: Saudi Arabia, Iran, Syria, Bahrain, Egypt, UAE, Kuwait, Malaysia, Indonesia, Singapore, Kenya, India, Cuba, China". One would think as a "Christian Nation", America would lead the world in protest to pornography instead of the promotion of pornography. These statistics say more about us as a society than we may choose to admit. The following statements were made by gospel preachers in different lectureships, and while I am not aware of their source of information, I accept their statements as true based upon the professionalism and honesty of these preachers. "Forty to sixty percent of all rapists view pornography to get charged up before going out to commit the crime" (B.J. Clarke, Sapulpa, Oklahoma, Lectures, 2004). "Ted Bundy, one day before his execution, stated, "without question, those inclined to serial murder all viewed pornography. Lots of other young people on the streets will be killed because of what they are viewing in the media" (Gary Summers, Spring, Texas, Lectures, 2005). Despite such testimony by criminals themselves, the US government continues to insist the individual has the right to participate in, and to promote that, which is detrimental and destructive to the welfare of others and society as a whole.

PORNOGRAPHY AND THE BIBLE

One may be surprised to learn that the word "pornography" does not appear in the Bible. But, the Bible has much to say about modesty and nudity. Before we look at these things, let's first define the meaning of our term, "por-nog-ra-phy, par-nog-ra-fe, n. [Gr: porne, prostitute, grapho, I write] literature or art calculated solely to supply sexual excitement; obscene literature or art. …" (WEBSTER, [p. 841). Two truths jump out at us in the definition of pornography.

First, literature can be just as pornographic as nudity. Second, certain art can also be classified as a form of pornography. A person does not have to be a rocket scientist to realize that nude art is not true art at all; it is nothing less than pornography. And, sexually explicit romance novels aren't novels at all but are nothing short of another form of pornography.

Pornography is referred to by its users as "eye candy". As we have already seen, those who are prone to commit sexual crimes turn to their "candy" before committing the crime. The defilement of Dinah, Jacob and Leah's daughter, by Shechem, is described in this manner, "And Dinah the daughter of Leah, which she bare unto Jacob, went out to see the daughters of the land. And when Shechem the son of Hamor the Hivite, prince of the country, saw her, he took her, and lay with her, and defiled her" (Gen. 34:1-2). Notice, he first "…saw her…" and then he "…took her…". Basically, the same thing transpired in the life of Joseph. But here, it was the woman who lusted after the man. The Bible says, "And it came to pass after these things, that his master's wife cast her eyes upon Joseph; and she said, Lie with me" (Gen. 39:7). Joseph, however, was a man of great integrity. He refused the advances of Potiphar's wife, although she stalked him daily, "And it came to pass, as she spake to Joseph day by day, that he hearkened not unto her, to lie by her, or to be with her" (Gen. 39:10). Joseph's reply to Potiphar's wife, as recorded in the latter part of verse nine was, "…how then can I do this great wickedness, and sin against God" (Gen. 39:9)? The best way to avoid a tragic situation like this is to flee from it, and this is exactly what Joseph did, "And she caught him by his garment, saying, Lie with me: and he left his garment in her hand, and fled, and got him out" (Gen. 39:12). If we ever hope to escape the clutches of pornography, or any other sin, we need to flee from and avoid it. As we see here, both men and women are vulnerable to its lure.

Jesus said, "Ye have heard that it was said by them of old time, Thou shalt not commit adultery: But I say unto you, That whosoever looketh on a woman to lust after her hath committed adultery with her already in his heart" (Matt. 5:27-28). Our Lord is not saying that it is a sin to recognize someone of the other gender as attractive, but it is a sin if, upon seeing them, we begin to formulate a plan in our heart to obtain them. James wrote, "But every man is tempted, when he is drawn away of his own lusts, and enticed. Then when lust had conceived, it bringeth forth sin: and sin, when it is finished, bringeth forth death" (Jam. 1:14-15). Please note, there is a distinction made between temptation and sin. The word "enticed" above means, "1185, deleazo, del-eh-ad-zo; from the base of 1388 dolos; to entrap, i.e. (fig.) delude: - allure, beguile, entice" (STRONG, p. 413 and 25). This same word appears in 2nd Peter 2:18 where it is translated "allure". Webster defines allure, "al-lure, a-lur, …To tempt by the offer of something good, real or apparent; to draw or try to draw by some purposed pleasure or advantage; to entice, decoy, tempt, charm, attract …" (29). Thus, to be attracted is the equivalent of being tempted. When one allows that attraction to lead them to make plans to satisfy their lust, lust has conceived and sin is then born in the heart. H. Leo Boles writes concerning this passage, "The thing which is condemned is not the look of admiration or affection, but the look of lust. As murder begins in the heart, so adultery begins in the heart. Jesus lays down a principle here which may be applied to both sexes. …The expression "looketh on a woman to lust after her" has the force of a cherished purpose. …The same manner of dealing with sin is manifest in the expression, "Whosoever hateth his brother is a murderer" (140). Not only is it a sin to lust after another, but it is just as sinful to contribute to that lust. Peter penned, "For the time past of our life may suffice us to have wrought the will of the Gentiles, when we walked in lasciviousness, lusts, excess of wine, revellings, banqueting, and abominable idolatries:" (1 Pet. 4:3). The World Book Dictionary defines lasciviousness, "lascivious (lesive es), adj. 1. inclined to or feeling lust: a lascivious person. 2. showing lust; lewd; wanton: He on Eve began to cast lascivious eyes (Milton). 3. causing lust or wantonness; …" (1181). For a person to display their nudity before others and to cause them to lust is as sinful and damnable as viewing nudity. Both parties are guilty of sin.

The Bible says that nakedness is shameful, "I counsel thee to buy of me gold tried in the fire, that thou mayest be rich; and white raiment, that thou mayest be clothed, and that the shame of thy nakedness do not appear; and anoint thy eyes with eye salve, that thou mayest see" (Rev. 3:18). This includes "so-called" art, as well as any other type of nakedness. Remember, Adam and Eve were called naked by the inspired book, even though they were partially clothed, "And the eyes of them both were opened, and they knew that they were naked; and they sewed fig leaves together, and made themselves aprons" (Gen. 3:7). "And the Lord God called unto Adam, and said unto him, where are thou? And he said, I heard thy voice in the garden, and I was afraid, because I was naked, and I hid myself" (Gen. 3:9-10). God apparently agreed with Adam, because the scripture then says, "Unto Adam also and unto his wife did the Lord God make coats of skins, and clothed them" (Gen. 3:21). Much of today's clothing is lewd, causing others to lust, and is as unacceptable to God as were the fig leaves of Adam and Eve. Sports Illustrated and other such magazines, as well as many television programs, and art galleries are nothing more than pornographic cesspools.

We would be lax if we did not include the "so-called" romantic novels in our discussion of pornography. This is a form of pornography which flies under the screen and is often overlooked. However, it is just as sinful to read about sexual promiscuity as it is to view it. Not only does Webster's definition of pornography include literature, the World Book Dictionary defines pornography, "pornography (por nog re fe), n. l. writings or pictures dealing with sexual matters in a manner intended to incite lust, …" (1623). Paul said, "But fornication, and all uncleanness, or covetousness, let it not be once named among you, as becometh saints; Neither filthiness, nor foolish talking, nor jesting, which are not convenient: but rather giving of thanks" (Eph. 5:3-4). And, "Abstain from all appearance of evil" (1 Thess. 5:22). And yet once again, "Who knowing the judgment of God, that they which commit such things are worthy of death, not only do the same, but have pleasure in them that do them" (Rom. 1:32). Finally, "And have no fellowship with the unfruitful works of darkness, but rather reprove them. For it is a shame even to speak of those things which are done of them in secret" (Eph. 5:11-12). I cannot imagine our Lord writing or reading such trash as this. They are overflowing with "uncleanness", "filthiness", and nasty innuendos. Furthermore, they too, just like nudity, incite others to lust. We have already pointed out this type of behavior is included and condemned in the sin of lasciviousness. Not only are we told not to partake of these sins, but to take pleasure in and to fellowship this type of activities is also wrong and unbecoming of a Christian. We must abstain from all appearances of evil and from fleshly lust which war against the soul, "Dearly beloved, I beseech you as strangers and pilgrims, abstain from fleshly lusts, which war against the soul;" (1 Pet. 2:11)

Pornography is also addictive and progressive. Those who have been enslaved to it report the desire to view it grows stronger after each visit. They also report their interest in more extreme types of sexual behavior increases too, such as in homosexuality, bestiality, pedophilia, and violent sexual activity. The wise man, Solomon, said, "All the labor of man is for his mouth, and yet the appetite is not filled" (Eccl. 6:7). This is true of the sex addict, too. They cannot get enough, although they tell themselves they can quit any time they decide to quit. Peter wrote of these,

But these, as natural brute beasts, made to be taken and destroyed, ...shall utterly perish in their own corruption; And shall receive the reward of unrighteousness, ...Spots they are and blemishes, sporting themselves with their own deceivings while they feast with you; Having eyes full of adultery, and that cannot cease from sin; beguiling unstable souls: a heart they have exercised with covetous practices; cursed children: (2 Pet. 2:12-14).

I am of the opinion this passage is talking about one's desire rather than his ability. Paul elsewhere states, "There hath no temptation taken you but such as is common to man: but God is faithful, who will not suffer you to be tempted above that ye are able; but will with the temptation also make a way to escape, that ye may be able to bear it" (1 Cor. 10:13). The danger exists in our desire, or lack of desire, to depart from the sin. The pleasure of sin can become so fulfilling to us we desire to experience this pleasure more than we desire to live eternally with God. Of this passage Adam Clark writes, "Cannot cease from sin] which ceases not from sin; they might cease from sin, but they do not; they love and practice it. Instead of, which cannot cease, several MSS. and versions have, and this requires the place to be read, Having eyes full of adultery and incessant sin" (888). Berry translates it thus, "eyes having full of adulteress, and that cease not from sin, alluring souls unestablished; a heart exercised in craving having, of curse children;" (605). This was the state of Israel when God spake to them through Jeremiah saying, "Can the Ethiopian change his skin, or the leopard his spots? then may ye also do good, that are accustomed to do evil" (Jer. 13:23). It was not the case that Israel could not change but she still was not willing to change. The same is true of so many today. Sin is so enjoyable to them they do not intend to leave it in order to please God.

ESCAPING SIN AND PORNOGRAPHY

We all have probably heard the old adage, "an ounce of prevention is worth a pound of cure". This is a true proverb. It is easier to never become involved with the practice of sin than it is to leave the practice of sin after we have tasted its pleasure. To avoid sexual temptation, Job said, "I have made a covenant with mine eyes; why then should I think upon a maid" (Job 31:1)? David likewise made a very similar statement, "I will set no wicked thing before mine eyes: I hate the work of them that turn aside; it shall not cleave to me" (Psa. 101:3). Perhaps after his ordeal with Bathsheba, David had learned to look the other way when temptation presented itself. Again, it has been said our eyes are windows to the soul. To protect and secure our soul we need to take heed to what we view. We need bridles for our tongues and blinders for our eyes.

Jesus taught the things which proceed out of the heart defile a man, "And he said, that which cometh out of a man, that defileth a man. For from within, out of the heart of men, proceed evil thoughts, adulteries, fornication, murders, thefts, covetousness, wickedness, deceit, lasciviousness, an evil eye, blasphemy, pride foolishness: All these evil things come from with in, and defile the man" (Mark 7:20-23). Thus, the wise man admonishes us to guard the heart, "Keep thy heart with all diligence; for out of it are the issues of life" (Prov. 4:23). Another old adage we are all probably familiar with is, "garbage in, garbage out". Again, this is a true proverb. The only way one can ever escape the sin of pornography, or any other sexual perversion, is to separate themselves from the sin and those people and things who are associated with it. Paul said, "Be not deceived: evil communications corrupt good manners. Awake to righteousness, and sin not: for some have not the knowledge of God: I speak this to your shame" (1 Cor. 15:33-34). This may mean we need to quit watching television and movies altogether. We may need to quit using the internet unless someone is nearby to supervise us. While these ends may seem extreme to some, it would be better to take these extreme measures than to spend an eternity in a devil's hell!

However, just to clean house is not enough. Jesus warned, "When the unclean spirit is gone out of a man, he walketh through dry places seeking rest, and findeth none. Then he saith, I will return into my house from whence I came out: and when he is come, he findeth it empty, swept, and garnished. Then goeth he, and taketh with himself seven other spirits more wicked than himself, and they enter in and dwell there: and the last state of that man is worse than the first. Even so shall it be also unto this wicked generation" (Matt. 12:43-45). Once our house has been cleaned, we need to replace the old practices of sin with works of righteousness or Satan will return to reclaim our souls. Let's replace valuable time spent viewing porn sights, movies, or reading romance novels with Bible study, "As newborn babes, desire the sincere milk of the word, that ye may grow thereby:" (1 Pet. 2:2). Instead of frequenting the bars and strip joints, let's attend all services, Bible studies, gospel meetings, lectureships, etc.;, not only of our congregation but of all those in our area, "Not forsaking the assembling of ourselves together, as the manner of some is; but exhorting one another: and so much the more, as ye see the day approaching:" (Hebrews 10:25). Instead of hanging out with old friends who encourage us to partake of these sins with them, let's busy ourselves in caring and tending to those in need and all other church programs where we can help, James said, "Pure religion and undefiled before God and the Father is this, to visit the fatherless and widows in their affliction, and to keep himself unspotted from the world" (Jam. 1:27). These are just a few helpful hints which can assist us in our battle against sin.

CONCLUSION

A Christian's attire is supposed to be modest, "In like manner also, that women adorn themselves in modest apparel, with shamefacedness and sobriety; not with braided hair, or gold, or pearls, or costly array; But (which becometh women professing godliness) with good works" (1 Tim. 2:9-10). Strong defines modest, "2887 Kosm'os, Kos-nee-os; from 2889 Kosmos (in its prim. sense); orderly, i.e. decorous; - of good behavior, modest" (STRONG, pgs. 922 and 56). If it is wrong to dress in such a way that it might incite lustful desires within others (lasciviousness), surely it is just as wrong to view those who wear such attire, or even less. Let us keep watch over ourselves that we be not taken in and deceived by Satan and the porn industry. As Paul said, "Finally brethren, whatsoever things are true, whatsoever things are honest, whatsoever things are just, whatsoever things are pure, whatsoever things are lovely, whatsoever things are of good report; if there be any virtue, and if there be any praise, think on these things" (Phil. 4:8).

STUDY QUESTIONS

1. Define moral.
2. Define pornography.
3. Are romantic novels a form of pornography?
4. Are nude drawings art or pornography?
5. What does it mean to look on a woman to lust after her (Matt. 5:27-28)?
6. Define lasciviousness.
7. Were Adam and Eve still considered naked in the eyes of God after they covered themselves with fig leaves?
8. Explain 2 Peter 2:14.
9. List five things we can do to help us overcome pornography.
10. Define modest.

END NOTES

1. All scripture quotations taken from the KJV of the Bible, unless otherwise noted.

2. The Living Webster Encyclopedia of the English Language, Noah Webster, The English Institute of America Inc., Chicago, Illinois, 1973, (p. 621).

3. www.familysafemedia.com/pornography_statistics.html.

4. The Living Webster Encyclopedia of the English Language, Noah Webster, The English Language Institute of America Inc., Chicago, Illinois, 1973, (p. 741).

5. Strong's Exhaustive Concordance of the Bible, James Strong, Thomas Nelson Publishers, Nashville - Camden - Kansas City, 1990, (pgs. 413 and 25).

6. The Living Webster Encyclopedia of the English Language, Noah Webster, The English Language Institute of America Inc., Chicago, Illinois, 1973 (p. 29).

7. The Gospel According to Matthew, H. Leo Boles, Gospel Advocate Co., Nashville, Tenn., 1979, (p. 140).

8. The World Book Dictionary, Volume Two L-Z, Edited by Clarence L. Barnhart, Robert K. Barnhart, World Book Inc., 1990, (p. 1181).

9. The World Book Dictionary, Volume Two L-Z, Edited by Clarence L. Barnhart, Robert K Barnhart, World Book Inc., 1990, (p. 1623).

10. Clarke's Commentary, Vol. VI, Romans - Revelation, Abingdon Press, New York - Nashville, copyright?, (p.888).

11. The Interlinear KJV, George Ricker Berry, Zondervan Publishing House, Grand Rapids, Michigan, copyright?, (p. 605).

12 Strong's Exhaustive Concordance of the Bible, James Strong, Thomas Nelson Publishers, Nashville - Camden - Kansas City, 1990, (pgs. 922 and 56).

DISHONESTY

Clint Yarber

INTRODUCTION

Christianity is an honest religion. Once we become a child of God we are to bid "adieu" to the shameful practice of dishonesty (2 Cor. 4:1-2). New Testament Christianity is to be an open, straight-forward religion. Thus, we do not deceive people into becoming Christians or being faithful members of the Lord's church. Our doctrines should be stated very clearly. Our beliefs should be openly proclaimed. We are not to be ashamed or afraid of what we believe and teach because our words and deeds are directed by the authority of Christ (Rom. 1:16-17; Col. 3:17).

One of the greatest challenges we face in Christianity is to keep ourselves pure (Jam. 1:27). Many so-called Christians today have allowed the immoral influence and practices of this world to rub off on them. The world has fashioned and molded their way of thinking, their words and their action so that it is difficult to tell the difference between those who profess to be Christians and those who do not. We must ever remember there is to be a very distinct moral line between the children of God and the children of Satan. We must be "…blameless and harmless, the sons of God, without rebuke, in the midst of a crooked and perverse nation, among whom ye shine as lights in the world" (Phil. 2:15).1 Whether we like it or not, the world is looking to us, and at us, as we live our lives. We must take care not to cause any to fall or stumble through immoral actions (Luke 17:1-2). Consequently, we are to "…provide things honest in the sight of all men" (Rom. 12:17), not just in our dealings with brothers and sisters in Christ. The influence and reputation of any Christian can be ruined by a single dishonest word or deed. Let's examine some Biblical teachings that will help us to remain moral people in the midst of a dishonest world.

SATAN, THE SOURCE OF DISHONESTY

The first thing we must understand about dishonesty is its origin. The roots of dishonesty go back to the story of the first man and woman. Jesus mentioned the source of dishonesty in a conversation He had with some Jews:

Ye are of your father the devil, and the lusts of your father ye will do. He was a murderer from the beginning, and abode not in the truth, because there is no truth in him. When he speaketh a lie, he speaketh of his own: for he is a liar, and the father of it (John 8:44).

Dishonesty has not come from God; in fact, it cannot (Tit. 1:2; Jam. 1:17). Its very origin and source comes to us from the mind of the most wicked being who has ever lived (Satan). It is hard to imagine the world in which we live, at one time knew no sin (Rom. 5:12). Dishonesty had never been spoken, or acted out, in the life of a single person. All that changed when Satan arrived upon the scene. He deliberately deceived Eve into eating of the tree of the knowledge of good and evil (Gen. 3:1-6). Notice the "subtlety" of the serpent is only mentioned in the Genesis account, but later on Paul would reveal, "...the serpent beguiled Eve through his subtilty..." (2 Cor. 11:3). It was through dishonest words and appeals that Satan brought the curse of sin and death upon the human race. Dishonesty led to man being separated from God (Isa. 59:1-2), and ultimately Jesus having to die upon the cross. Nothing good comes from dishonesty. These facts, in and of themselves, should be enough to keep us away from every dishonest act and word.

FORMS OF DISHONESTY

There are many different forms of dishonesty that exist in the world today. Some of these points either have been, or will be, discussed in other lessons of this book. This being the case, I will not devote a great deal of attention to them, knowing the reader can find a fuller discussion of them elsewhere in the book.

Stealing

It should go without saying the Bible specifically forbids the unlawful taking of that which belongs to someone else. God's word abounds with such direct commands: "Thou shalt not steal" (Ex. 20:15).

> Owe no man any thing, but to love one another: for he that loveth another hath fulfilled the law. For this, Thou shalt not commit adultery, Thou shalt not kill, Thou shalt not steal, Thou shalt not bear false witness, Thou shalt not covet; and if there be any other commandment, it is briefly comprehended in this saying, namely, Thou shalt love thy neighbour as thyself (Rom. 13:8-9).

> Let him that stole steal no more: but rather let him labour, working with his hands the thing which is good, that he may have to give to him that needeth (Eph. 4:28).

While many Christians would never dream of directly taking somebody else's property, not all stealing is committed in a direct manner. Some today are guilty of stealing from God.

> Will a man rob God? Yet ye have robbed me. But ye say, Wherein have we robbed thee? In tithes and offerings. Ye are cursed with a curse: for ye have robbed me, even this whole nation (Mal. 3:8-9).

Whenever we withhold from our offering what rightfully belongs to God, we are guilty of dishonesty. We have taken that which belongs to God and used it for ourselves. How many of us would walk up to the collection plate after services, pull out a big wad of cash and stick it in our pockets? We cringe in horror at such a thought! Yet such an act would be no more dishonest than withholding what should be given to God.

We can be guilty of stealing time from God too. As Christians we are to "...walk circumspectly, not as fools, but as wise, redeeming the time, because the days are evil" (Eph. 5:15-16). When we take time that is supposed to be given to God and use it for ourselves, we have stolen from the very hand that feeds us. This dishonesty exists in the form of forsaking the assembly:

> Not forsaking the assembling of ourselves together, as the manner of some is; but exhorting one another: and so much the more, as ye see the day approaching (Heb. 10:25).

When we do not give God the time that belongs to Him upon any day of the week, we have stolen from Him. This same principle can be applied in Bible study, prayer, good deeds, etc. If we do not use the time God has given us for our appointed purposes, we become guilty of stealing from Him and thus dishonest in our actions.

We can also steal from God by not using the talents He has given us (Matt. 25:14-30). Since our talents rightfully belong to Him (Matt. 35:14; 1 Cor. 4:1-2), we are to use them in the way He has authorized. If a man can lead a song and he does not do so, he has taken what belongs to God (stealing) and buried it in the earth (Matt. 25:25). Anyone who has the ability to preach the Gospel, be an elder, serve as a deacon or direct a Bible class and does not use that talent; he/she is a dishonest individual. Why? Because they have taken that which God has entrusted into their care and not used it. Such actions are dishonest!

We cannot only be guilty of stealing from God, but also from our fellow man. Whenever we go about our daily jobs, we should put in an honest day's work for an honest day's pay (Rom. 12:17). We have a contract with our employer we will work an hour for so many dollars or do so much work for so much money. Many people do fine as long as the boss is within sight, but what happens when he is not around? Some find no harm in "loafing" if no one is watching. Someone is watching and the someone is God! Such actions are dishonest in nature and nothing short of stealing. Other such dishonesty exists in the form of taking longer breaks than allowed or maybe even squeezing a few more minutes out of your lunch hour. All these are forms of stealing.

Copyright stealing is another form of dishonesty. Downloading or copying music or movies for which one has not paid is nothing short of stealing. We have laws in this land that forbid such actions. God has decreed we are to obey the laws of our land as long as they do not oppose His laws (Rom. 13:1-2; Acts 5:29). If the laws of the land state such actions are dishonest and illegal, how should the Christian feel toward them? These are just a few of the forms of dishonesty that exist in the form of stealing.

Lying

Another form of dishonesty falls under the heading of lying. I will not devote a great deal of space to this subject, because it is specifically addressed in another chapter. Nevertheless, it is a form of dishonesty. Just like stealing, lying is also directly forbidden by God's laws, "Wherefore putting away lying, speak every man truth with his neighbour: for we are members one of another" (Eph. 4:25). "Lie not one to another, seeing that ye have put off the old man with his deeds;" (Col. 3:9).

> Again, ye have heard that it hath been said by them of old time, Thou shalt not forswear thyself, but shalt perform unto the Lord thine oaths: But I say unto you,

> Swear not at all; neither by heaven; for it is God's throne: Nor by the earth; for it is his footstool: neither by Jerusalem; for it is the city of the great King. Neither shalt thou swear by thy head, because thou canst not make one hair white or black. But let your communication be, Yea, yea; Nay, nay: for whatsoever is more than these cometh of evil (Matt. 5:33-37).

Once again the child of God might never look into someone's eye and tell them a bold faced lie, but lying is not always done in a direct manner. In fact, we can even be guilty of lying to ourselves. Consider the following verses:

> But be ye doers of the word, and not hearers only, deceiving your own selves (Jam. 1:22).
>
> Be not deceived; God is not mocked: for whatsoever a man soweth, that shall he also reap (Gal. 6:7).
>
> Let no man deceive himself. If any man among you seemeth to be wise in this world, let him become a fool, that he may be wise (1 Cor. 3:18).
>
> For if a man think himself to be something, when he is nothing, he deceiveth himself (Gal. 6:3).
>
> If we say that we have no sin, we deceive ourselves, and the truth is not in us (1 John 1:8).
>
> He that saith, I know him, and keepeth not his commandments, is a liar, and the truth is not in him (1 John 2:4).
>
> If a man say, I love God, and hateth his brother, he is a liar: for he that loveth not his brother whom he hath

> seen, how can he love God whom he hath not seen? (1 John 4:20).

A host of other Scriptures could be added to the above, but suffice it to say that we as Christians should be careful we do not lie to ourselves or anybody else! It is a dishonest practice.

Cheating

Cheating is yet one more form of dishonesty that exists in the world today. Once again, there are many avenues through which a person can become guilty of this sin. Not paying our taxes is one form that comes to mind. The Bible clearly teaches us that we are to give tribute to our government, no matter how corrupt and ungodly the government may be.

> Then went the Pharisees, and took counsel how they might entangle him in his talk. And they sent out unto him their disciples with the Herodians, saying, Master, we know that thou art true, and teachest the way of God in truth, neither carest thou for any man: for thou regardest not the person of men. Tell us therefore, What thinkest thou? Is it lawful to give tribute unto Caesar, or not? But Jesus perceived their wickedness, and said, Why tempt ye me, ye hypocrites? Shew me the tribute money. And they brought unto him a penny. And he saith unto them, Whose is this image and superscription? They say unto him, Caesar's. Then saith he unto them, Render therefore unto Caesar the things which are Caesar's; and unto God the things that are God's (Matt. 22:15-21).

> For this cause pay ye tribute also: for they are God's ministers, attending continually upon this very thing. Render therefore to all their dues: tribute to whom tribute is due; custom to whom custom; fear to whom fear; honour to whom honour (Rom. 13:6-7).

It is up to the Christian to see we give tribute where it is due, but it is up to the government to see they use the tribute money in the proper way. We must do our part even if the higher powers do not do theirs! When we fail to do such, we become guilty of dishonesty.

Business transactions are another area in which one can be dishonest. Even children of God are not immune to the temptation to gain an advantage through buying, trading or selling. Some will advertise a product for better, or more, than what it really is. The nation of Israel became guilty of the sin of cheating:

> Hear this, O ye that swallow up the needy, even to make the poor of the land to fail, Saying, When will the new moon be gone, that we may sell corn? and the sabbath, that we may set forth wheat, making the ephah small, and the shekel great, and falsifying the balances by deceit? That we may buy the poor for silver, and the needy for a pair of shoes; yea, and sell the refuse of the wheat? (Amos 8:4-6).

God's own people had "tipped the scales" in their favor. Such practices are ungodly and dishonest in nature. A store manager once heard his clerk tell a customer, "No, ma'am, we have not had any for a while, and it does not look as if we will be getting any soon." Horrified, the manager came running over to the customer and said, "Of course we will have some soon. We placed an order last week." Then the manager drew the clerk aside. "Never," he snarled, "Never, never, never say we are out of anything. Say we have got it on order and it is coming. Now, what was it she wanted anyway?" The clerk said, "Rain!" While the above illustration is humorous in nature, it shows the dishonest lengths to which some will go to keep people coming back. They will lie and manipulate the truth in order to gain a financial advantage. This is certainly a dishonest practice and one that has no place within the life of a Christian.

Another form of "cheating" can be found within the realm of marriage. Whenever God joins a man and a woman in marriage, they are in a life-long covenant that can only be broken by one act—fornication (Matt. 19:9). Under the Law of Moses, the Jews had forgotten the significance of this covenant they made with their spouses:

> Yet ye say, Wherefore? Because the Lord hath been witness between thee and the wife of thy youth, against whom thou hast dealt treacherously: yet is she thy companion, and the wife of thy covenant. And did not he make one? Yet had he the residue of the spirit. And wherefore one? That he might seek a godly seed. Therefore take heed to your spirit, and let none deal treacherously against the wife of his youth (Mal. 2:14-15).

The covenant of marriage includes reserving our bodies for our mate and our mate only. Whenever we enter into the marriage covenant, we have vowed to keep ourselves to one person until death separates us. Many people today have forgotten the covenant they made with their spouse. Maybe "forgotten" is not the correct word; "forsaken" would be much more appropriate. They "cheat" on their mate by giving their bodies to someone else. Not only can the sin of adultery fall under the category of cheating, but it also fits within the realm of stealing. Paul wrote:

> Let the husband render unto the wife due benevolence: and likewise also the wife unto the husband. The wife hath not power of her own body, but the husband: and likewise also the husband hath not power of his own body, but the wife. Defraud ye not one the other, except it be with consent for a time, that ye may give yourselves to fasting and prayer; and come together again, that Satan tempt you not for your incontinency (1 Cor. 7:3-5).

When we deprive our spouses of what rightfully belongs to them, we have become guilty of theft. Whether we categorize adultery as stealing or cheating, either way it is a dishonest practice which has no place in the life of a faithful Christian.

WHY DO SOME PRACTICE DISHONESTY?

Having considered some of the different forms of dishonesty, we now turn our attention to the "why" of dishonesty.

Some people practice dishonesty because they have never faced any consequences from it. The wise man spoke of this very principle in the book of Ecclesiastes: "Because sentence against an evil work is not executed speedily, therefore the heart of the sons of men is fully set in them to do evil" (Ecc. 8:11).

Many today think they have gotten away with dishonesty because it is something that happened many years ago. While it may have escaped the attention of men, yet it has not gone unnoticed by God. We will give an account of every dishonest word and act we have performed upon this earth (Matt. 12:36-37; 2 Cor. 5:10).

Others practice dishonesty because they are greedy individuals (Amos 8:4-6). The Bible certainly has much to say about the subject of greed and its consequences (Luke 12:15; 1 Cor. 6:10; 1 Tim. 6:9-10).

Still more practice dishonesty to appear "bigger" than what they really are. Ananias and Sapphira are a prime example of such. They lied about how much they had given, perhaps to appear more righteous or spiritually minded in the eyes of men (Acts 5:1-10).

Aaron practiced dishonesty in order to lessen the guilt of his actions: "And I said unto them, Whosoever hath any gold, let them break it off. So they gave it me: then I cast it into the fire, and there came out this calf" (Ex. 32:24). Who, in their right mind would believe this statement? Yet, how many men today tell some of the most outrageous lies in an attempt to lessen the consequences of their actions?

Regardless of why one chooses to practice dishonesty, it is never right in the sight of God. While the world may deem these as good reasons to be dishonest, God does not!

CONCLUSION

All of the consequences of dishonesty are too numerous to list in this lesson. But dishonesty will destroy nations (Prov. 14:34) and relationships (Pharaoh and Abraham; Jacob and Esau, etc.). But the most important relationship it will affect is our relationship with God. Dishonesty is a sin, and sin; any sin can separate us from God for all of eternity (Isa. 59:1-2; Rev. 21:8). Christianity is an honest religion! Let us all do our very best to say goodbye to the shameful, immoral and eternally hurtful sin of dishonesty (2 Cor. 4:1-2).

STUDY QUESTIONS

1. What type of religion is Christianity?
2. From where has dishonesty come?
3. What did Satan use to help usher sin into this world?
4. List three different types of dishonesty.
5. What are some different forms of stealing?
6. How does lying fit into the category of dishonesty?
7. Discuss the different manners of cheating.
8. Why do some people practice dishonesty?
9. Discuss the statement, "Dishonesty does not always come in a direct form."
10. What are some of the consequences of dishonesty?

ENDNOTES

1. All quotations are taken from the King James Version unless otherwise stated.

IMMORAL SPEECH

Melvin L. Otey

INTRODUCTION

Of all the various members of the human body, few are of greater concern to God than the tongue, which, by metonymy, usually represents our speech in Scripture. For example, two of the ten commandments given to the children of Israel addressed their speech: "Thou shalt not take the name of the LORD thy God in vain; for the LORD will not hold him guiltless that taketh his name in vain," and "Thou shalt not bear false witness against thy neighbour" (Ex. 20:7, 16). Twenty percent of the Decalogue, then, might be summarized thusly: "Watch your mouth. Control your tongue."

The importance God places on human speech is further demonstrated by the attention given the matter in the book of Proverbs. The tongue is one of its oft referenced subjects (see, e.g., Prov. 6:12; 10:18-21, 31-32; 11:9, 13; 12:13, 18-19, 22-23; 13:3, 5; 20:19). For example, of the seven abominations to the Lord listed in Proverbs 6:16-19, three are a lying tongue, a false witness that speaks lies, and sowing discord among brethren. One of the dominant themes in the book of wise sayings, then, is, "Watch your mouth. Control your tongue."

The Bible's call to disciplined, savory speech is especially important for the Christian. In the same way that a linguistic accent reveals one's geographic background, linguistic content reveals his spiritual background, whether he has been feasting at the feet of the Lord or filling his belly with swine in the "far country" with God-less "Gentiles." The tongue often tells whose we are as soon as we open our mouths, whether we serve Christ or "the god of this world" (2

Cor. 4:4). It is imperative, therefore, that the Christian's speech is upright, befitting of his relationship with God.

Because God has always been especially concerned with the speech of those who represent Him, we are not surprised that His deep interest is continually expressed in the New Testament (see, e.g., Mt. 5:22; Jn. 8:44; Col. 3:8; Eph. 4:29, 5:4; Rom. 12:14; 1 Pet. 3:10). Also, it is noteworthy that the book of James offers a particularly extensive treatment. The Lord's brother mentioned the tongue in each chapter of his epistle (1:19, 1:26, 2:12, 3:1-12, 4:11, 5:12) and offered a lengthy discussion in chapter three, where we find the passage of our immediate emphasis.

AN EXPANSIVE PROBLEM (3:1-2)

James wrote to Christians who had been scattered abroad because of the persecution that was so prevalent in the infancy of the church (Jam. 1:1; Acts 8:1). "My brethren, be not many masters," he cautioned, "knowing that we shall receive the greater condemnation" (Jam. 3:1). This verse merits extensive treatment of its own, but suffice it to say here that the gravamen of James' warning was that men must carefully count the cost before putting themselves, or allowing others to put them, into position to teach and lead others concerning the things of God and the duties of man.

The Greek construction is written in the present imperative (Burdick 186), suggesting there was an established problem with teachers esteeming the responsibility too lightly or embracing it prematurely. Of course, saints are called to teach the will of God to Christians and non-Christians alike (Mt. 28:19-20; Tit. 2:3-4; 2 Tim. 2:2), but the work must be undertaken with sobriety and gravity because teachers will receive the "greater condemnation," or the "stricter judgment" (NKJV). Those who are responsible to know more, and purport to know more, will be scrutinized more closely by

God, and also by man, in part, because their greater influence magnifies their potential for doing harm (cf. Rom. 2:21-24).

After announcing his specific concern about teachers, James transitioned to a broader proposition, the one that concerns us here. "For in many things we offend all" (Jam. 3:2a). Some of the newer translations are perhaps more clear. The New King James Version says, "We all stumble in many things." The New American Standard Bible says, "We all stumble in many ways." Everyone falters in walking with the Lord at some point (Rom. 3:10, 23). More specifically, though, everyone falters in his speech: "If any man offend not in word, the same is a perfect man and able also to bridle the whole body" (Jam. 3:2b). Sins of the tongue are hardest to avoid, so the one who can control his speech can likely control himself in every respect.

Restraining the tongue from evil is not the challenge of a select few. Nor is it a challenge from which a blessed minority is exempt. The physical tongue "is more sensitive to touch, temperature, and pain than any other part of the body" (Balaban and Bobick 142). It is, therefore, an apropos representative for our speech. More than being an essential part of producing words, it has the volatile, reactive quality we sometimes manifest with our words. James, a pillar within the influential Jerusalem church (Gal. 2:9), counted himself among those who sometimes struggled in this area: "In many things we offend all" (emphasis added). The problem of controlling our speech is, indeed, universal.

AN INFLUENTIAL PART (3:3-5)

While it is not necessarily an easy task, controlling one's speech is absolutely imperative because our speech is very influential. James affirmed this point with two illustrations. First, he referenced horses, powerful beasts that weigh hundreds of pounds and can move as fast as automobiles. When encountered in the wild, they are difficult and dangerous to control. Yet, men have learned to direct their conduct by placing small pieces of metal, called bits, into their mouths. "Behold we put bits in the horses' mouths, that they may obey us; and we turn about their whole body" (Jam. 3:3). We can curb their rebellious spirits and channel their explosive power simply by manipulating their little tongues.

In the second illustration, James wrote, "Behold also ships, which though they be so great, and are driven by fierce winds, yet are they turned about with a very small helm, whithersoever the governor listeth" (Jam. 3:4). Here, again, ships are large and powerful. Moreover, they are heavily affected by external forces like fierce winds, but they are ultimately controlled by a small device called a helm. This device determines the entire vessel's course. No captain can stop the storms and the winds, but, even in their midst, he can still steer his ship in the direction he chooses.

"Even so the tongue is a little member, and boasteth great things" (Jam. 3:5). The physical tongue is only a small part of a man's physical body, but its influence on his spiritual course is disproportionately profound, like a bit in a horse's mouth or the helm of a ship. Indeed, "Death and life are in the power of the tongue" (Prov. 18:21a). Our tongues are like wild horses that must be controlled. Our lives are like ships at sea enduring tempestuous storms and fierce winds. If we do not steer carefully, we will be blown off course, but, in the midst of it all, our speech largely determines our course, either toward everlasting salvation or toward eternal damnation.

The dramatic influence of this small member is somewhat startling. "Even so the tongue is a little member, and boasteth great things. Behold, how great a matter a little fire kindleth!" (Jam. 3:5). Only a little spark is required to burn down an entire forest. One camper forgets to extinguish his small cooking fire and, soon thereafter, the nation watches as a blaze rages across several states and consumes thousands of precious acres. The tongue is small, but its influence is potentially enormous like the potential influence of a little fire.

AN IMMORAL POTENTIAL (3:6-8)

A small spark from the tongue can have the same deadly affect as a small spark from a match. A thoughtless remark can also start a big fire. A tiny expression of malice can also cause a huge explosion. With the tongue, wars begin, marriages end, and reputations are destroyed. It really is no wonder, then, that James described the tongue as "a fire" and "a world of iniquity" (Jam. 3:6a). Like a little spark in a forest of dry timber, "so is the tongue among our members, that it defileth the whole body, and setteth on fire the course of nature; and it is set on fire of hell" (Jam. 3:6b). There is an endless universe of ways for us to stumble and fall into immorality based on our speech alone. So then, if we do not control our tongues, our entire beings can quickly be consumed, ablaze in sin. Solomon solemnly warned, "Suffer not thy mouth to cause thy flesh to sin" (Eccl. 5:6a).

James wrote to encourage Christians to safeguard their speech, while acknowledging that it is a daunting task because the tongue is "an unruly evil" and "full of deadly poison" (Jam. 3:8b). Every kind of beast, bird, serpent, and creature in the sea, he observed, has been tamed by man, "But the tongue can no man tame" (Jam. 3:8a). Again, the problem truly is universal. Though the tongue cannot be tamed, or completely domesticated, it can, and must, be controlled because the potential for immoral speech is virtually boundless.

For example, immoral speech includes lying, which is "abomination to the LORD" (Prov. 12:22). Lying is of the devil (Jn. 8:44), yet even great men like Abraham and Isaac sometimes struggled to maintain their veracity (Gen. 12:11-20, 20:1-13, 26:6-9). We are no better than they were. We must never forget that deceptive and dishonest speech will actually keep some from sharing a home in heaven with God (Rev. 21:8, 27). Clearly, anything that can potentially cost a person his or her salvation is "full of deadly poison," and dishonest speech can cost us that much.

Immoral speech also includes gossiping, murmuring, backbiting, and tale bearing, various forms of spewing negative things in a private, hurtful manner. Such behavior certainly reflects poorly on the purveyor. "Gossip and trashy talk undercut our ability to communicate well, communicate with credibility, and communicate positively to change our world" (Chaddock 166). Such behavior is also harmful to others. On two occasions, the Bible says, "The words of a talebearer are as wounds, and they go down into the innermost parts of the belly" (Prov. 18:8; 26:22). Words can penetrate places that material weapons could never reach. Anything that has a propensity to hurt our influence for Christ and severely injure others can fairly be characterized as "full of deadly poison," and ungodly speech can sometimes wound more severely than a gun or a knife.

The tongue is "full of deadly poison" because it is used to introduce vulgarity and unsavory jokes. Unfortunately, we sometimes use coarse language to get attention or emphasize a point that is important to us. This is obviously immoral because Ephesians 5:4 says "neither filthiness, nor foolish talking, nor jesting, which are not convenient" should be named once among Christians. Proverbs 17:5 teaches that making fun of the poor is akin to reproach and blasphemy of God Almighty. All hateful, distasteful speech is evil, even when it is disguised as "honesty" or "humor" (Col. 3:8).

The tongue is "full of deadly poison" because hypocritical (Prov. 11:9; 1 Tim. 4:2), perverse (Prov. 4:24, 17:20, 19:1), flattering (Psa. 12:3; Prov. 20:19, 26:28), slanderous (Psa. 101:5; Prov. 10:18; Jam. 4:11), foolish (Prov. 18:6-7), and boastful speech (Prov. 27:2; Dan. 4:28-37) often enter the world through it. Yet, one of the most vulgar abuses of the tongue, of the instrument that God has given us for broadcasting His message to the world, is cursing (Jam. 3:9-10). The term "cursing" is commonly used with reference to profanity today, but its original meaning includes blasphemy and wishing evil on another (cf. Lk. 6:28; Lev. 24:15-16). There are many ways to transgress God's will with our speech, and God will be displeased with them all. Maintaining our spiritual purity requires vigilant attention to our tongues.

AN EFFECTIVE PLAN

The potential for immoral speech is seemingly limitless, but every one of us must control our tongues because "Therewith bless we God, even the Father" (Jam. 3:9). The tongue is an instrument given to us by God for His praise, so it is always wrong to use it in a manner inconsistent with His will. James asked, "Doth a fountain send forth at the same place sweet water and bitter? Can the fig tree, my brethren, bear olive berries? either a vine, figs?" The obvious answer to these questions is, "No, it does not. No, it cannot." God has given us "all things that pertain unto life and godliness" (2 Pet. 1:3), and His Word gives us instructions for refraining from immoral speech.

The first thing one must do is set his mind to do better because the mind controls the tongue (Mt. 12:34-35). Job said, "All the while my breath is in me, and the spirit of God is in my nostrils; My lips shall not speak wickedness, nor my tongue utter deceit" (Job 27:3-4). Moreover, note the resolve of David, who said, "I am purposed that my mouth shall not transgress" (Psa. 17:3), and "I said, I will take heed to my ways, that I sin not with my tongue: I will keep my mouth with a bridle, while the wicked is before me" (Psa. 39:1). The tongue resides in a wet place; it can slip easily, so precautions have to be taken. One must resolve each day to "Let no corrupt communication proceed out of your mouth, but that which is good to the use of edifying, that it may minister grace unto the hearers" (Eph. 4:29).

This may seem antithetical to many, but the second step in quelling immoral speech is closing our mouths. Many things are opened by mistake, but none so frequently as the mouth. We have to "stop the bleeding," so to speak. "In the multitude of words there wanteth not sin: but he that refraineth his lips is wise" (Prov. 10:19). "He that keepeth his mouth keepeth his life: but he that openeth wide his lips shall have destruction" (Prov. 13:3). "Even a fool, when he holdeth his peace, is counted wise: and he that shutteth his lips is esteemed a man of understanding" (Prov. 17:28). In other words, it is better to remain silent and be thought a fool, than to open your mouth and remove all doubt. God has not given this counsel in vain. We can go a long way toward avoiding immorality by simply keeping our mouths closed.

Third, it is imperative that we pray that God will help us with our tongues. James was abundantly clear: "The tongue can no man tame" (Jam. 3:8). Prayer is always a great place to start in dealing with our weaknesses (see, e.g., Jam. 1:5; 1 Kgs. 3:9-10). We might echo the Psalmists' prayers, "Set a watch, O LORD, before my mouth; keep the door of my lips" (Psa. 141:3), and "Let the words of my mouth, and the meditation of my heart, be acceptable in thy sight, O LORD, my strength, and my redeemer" (Psa. 19:14). We need God's help to keep us from ungodliness of every kind, including immoral speech.

Fourth, if we want to improve our speech, we have to refine our hearts. "We can be sure that whatever is in our hearts will eventually spill out of our spouts" (Gilpin 57). Immoral speech comes out of our mouths because we sometimes harbor immoral attitudes in our hearts. Our Lord said, "A good man out of the good treasure of the heart bringeth forth good things: and an evil man out of the evil treasure bringeth forth evil things" (Mt. 12:35). Therefore, if we do not bring forth evil speech, we must saturate our minds with the good things we find in Scripture. The Word of God will convert our souls and renew our minds (Psa. 19:7). Remember, "Thy word have I hid in mine heart, that I might not sin against thee" (Psa. 119:11). It is futile to attempt to control the tongue without first subduing the mind with the Bible.

Fifth, we must listen carefully before deciding whether it is even appropriate to speak. "He that answereth a matter before he heareth it, it is folly and shame unto him" (Prov. 18:13). "Wherefore my beloved brethren, let every man be swift to hear, slow to speak, slow to wrath" (Jam. 1:19). Instead of broadcasting so much, we can avoid immoral speech by tuning in more carefully and consistently.

Lastly, when we find it necessary to speak, we must choose our words very carefully. "That words are powerful may seem obvious, but the fact is that most of us, most of the time, use them lightly. We choose our clothes more carefully than we choose our Words . . ." (Telushkin 4). We cannot unring a bell, unsing a song, undo a deed, or unspeak a word. Communication is irreversible. If something needs to be said, measure twice, cut once. "Seest thou a man that is hasty in his words? There is more hope for a fool than of him" (Prov. 29:20). Again, the Bible says, "It is a snare to say rashly, 'It is holy,' and to reflect only after making vows" (Prov. 20:25 ESV).

Before we speak our minds, we should be certain that what we propose to say is true, necessary, measured, helpful and kind. Remember, "Pleasant words are as an honeycomb, sweet to the soul, and health to the bones" (Prov. 16:24), and "A word fitly spoken is like apples of gold in pictures of silver" (Prov. 25:11). We never want to harm someone else with our words, and it is very easy to do so, but we should never miss an opportunity to encourage and edify others. Whenever we speak, let our speech be "always seasoned with salt" (Col. 4:6).

CONCLUSION

In Isaiah 6:5, the prophet said, "I am a man of unclean lips and I live among a people of unclean lips." We can truly echo these words, and we are all responsible to be ever diligent to avoid ungodly speech. What then do we propose to do? We should repent, purpose in our hearts to do better, confess our shortcomings, entreat God to forgive us and help us, and, ultimately, just do better. Make no mistake. The stakes are high. We will give account to God for every word we have ever spoken, and he knows every word that falls from our lips (Mt. 12:36-37; Psa. 139:4; cf. Eccl. 12:14). This is a sobering thought. Truly, "Whoso keepeth his mouth and his tongue keepeth his soul from troubles" (Prov. 21:23). Remember, "If any man seem to be religious and bridleth not his tongue, but deceiveth his own heart, this man's religion is in vain" (Jam. 1:26).

STUDY QUESTIONS

1. How has God manifested His special concern with our speech?
2. In what respects is the tongue an appropriate representative for our speech?
3. What illustrations did James use to demonstrate the profound influence of our speech?
4. Why did James describe the tongue as "an unruly evil" and "full of deadly poison"?
5. What are some common types of immoral speech that plague us?
6. What are some biblical examples of otherwise godly people who exhibited immoral speech?
7. For what purpose has God designed the tongue (as it pertains to our speech)?
8. What is the first key to avoiding immoral speech?
9. What is the relationship between our tongues and our hearts?
10. Why is it critical to think very carefully before we speak?

WORKS CITED

Balaban, Naomi and James Bobick. The Handy Anatomy Answer Book. Detroit: Visible Ink, 2008.

Burdick, Donald W. "James." The Expositor's Bible Commentary. Ed. Frank Gaebelein. Grand Rapids: Zondervan, 1981.

Chaddock, Robin. How to Get a Smart Mouth. Eugene: Harvest House, 2008.

Flynn, Claude. "James 3:1-12: The Proper and Improper Use of the Tongue." Great Texts of the Bible Revisited. Eds. Floyd Bailey, Jr., Mark A. Howell, and Allen Webster. Montgomery: Faulkner University, 1993.

Gilpin, Jeanny. "What's Pouring Out of Our Spout?" Christian Woman. September/October 2008:57.

Telushkin, Joseph. Words That Hurt Words That Heal. New York: William Morrow, 1996.

Tucker, Karen. "A Word Fitly Spoken." West Virginia Christian. August 2011:5.

MATERIALISM

Bobby Liddell

> Love not the world, neither the things that are in the world. If any man love the world, the love of the Father is not in him. For all that is in the world, the lust of the flesh, and the lust of the eyes, and the pride of life, is not of the Father, but is of the world. And the world passeth away, and the lust thereof: but he that doeth the will of God abideth for ever (1 John 2:15-17).

INTRODUCTION

Materialism is the concept that the things that are physical (material) are of highest importance, and that love for, enjoyment of, and pursuit of the "things" of the world should be the dominant objective, and rule of life for man. Therefore, materialism contends those things that are spiritual (and eternal) are not most important, and are not what man should seek, nor about which man should be concerned.

Consider the problems of the materialistic contention for loving the things of this world. Love of the world robs one of fellowship with the Father (1 John 1:6-10; Isa. 59:1-2; 1 John 5:3; Rev. 22:14). Love of the world robs one of heaven, by emphasizing the "here and now," instead of the hereafter (Rev. 14:13; Heb. 9:27; Jam. 4:14). Love of the world robs one of that which is most valuable--his soul (Mat. 16:26; 25:46; Rev. 21:27).

Consider the prevalence of the materialistic custom of loving the world. The majority of people love the world (Mat. 7:13-14).

Sadly, many have known no other way of life (Rom. 10:13-17). Sadder still, many who do know better, want no other way, and choose to love the world (cf. Josh. 24:15). Saddest of all, regardless of knowledge, love of the world disappoints and destroys (Luke 15:11-ff). Worldliness is a prevalent sin, but should not be (Tit. 2:11-12; 1 John 5:4). Even the Lord's church has been affected by materialistic members' love of the world (cf. 2 Tim. 4:10), but love of the world will cause a man to rob God (Mal. 3:8; 1 Cor. 16:1-2). Love of the world will cause a man to forsake the assembly (Heb. 10:25). Love of the world will cause a man to be self-centered instead of Christ-centered; pleasure seeking instead of soul seeking; and, worldly instead of godly (Mat. 6:33; Luke 9:23-24; Mat. 28:18-20; Tit. 2:11-12).

MATERIALISM AND LOVING THE WORLD THE LOVE OF THE WORLD

(1 John 2:15). John penned: "Love not the world." The "world" is a reference to that which is ungodly, wicked, and sinful--the system or order of worldliness as characterized by the lusts here mentioned. John's reference to the world is not to God's material creation, nor to the people who inhabit it. There is a sense in which we must love the "world"; that is, the souls of the people of the world (John 3:16; 1:29; Mark 16:15-16); however, our affections are not to be centered on the sinful activities and associations of this world (2 Cor. 6:14-7:1).

We must not love the things in the world. The "things" refer to the individual and particular aspects of the wicked world. We must not love the world in general, nor the things of it in particular, for these are not of the Father. Thus, there is not one thing of the wicked world we should love (1 Cor. 6:9-11; Luke 12:15; 1 Tim. 6:10).

Why would anyone love things? Some want possessions. Some want power. Some want popularity. Some want pleasure, and the things of the world bring pleasure. Without pleasure, sin would lose its appeal (Heb. 3:13); however, the pleasure of sin is fleeting and momentary (Heb. 11:25). Often, the pleasures of sin blind one to his movement away from God and his love of God.

We must love the Father. One cannot love both the world and the Father. If one loves the world, he cannot love the Father (Mat. 6:24). If one loves the Father, he cannot love the world (Mat. 22:37). If one loves the Father, he will keep His commandments, one of which is, "Love not the world" (1 John 5:3; 2:15).

Why love the Father? We love God because He first loved us (1 John 4:19). We love God because of what He has done for us (John 3:16; Rom. 5:8-9), and has made possible for us (1 John 3:1-2). In view of this, the question should be: "Why not love the Father?" If one loves the Father, he will not take part in the wickedness of worldly materialism by making close companions of the worldly (1 Cor. 15:33; Psa. 1:1-2). He will not seek to think like, be like, look like, or talk like the world. He will want to be the friend of God, not of the world (Jam. 4:4).

THE LUSTS OF THE WORLD

1 John 2:16, includes the lust of the flesh. Lust refers to desire. In this case, the object is the fulfillment of illicit desire, or the fulfillment of lawful desire in an unlawful way or degree (Jam. 1:13-15). The lust of the flesh is the desire for that which appeals to the flesh (Gal. 5:19-21). Satan tempted Eve (who saw the tree was good for food), and Jesus, by appealing to the lust of the flesh (Gen. 3:6; Mat. 4:1-4).

The lusts of the world include the lust of the eyes. In the Garden, the fruit of the forbidden tree was "pleasant to the eyes" of Eve (Gen. 3:6). Likewise, Satan appealed to Jesus to look at all the kingdoms of the world (and the glory of them) that he promised to give to Jesus (Mat. 4:8). Like Achan, many see the world and its things and lust after them, though forbidden (Josh. 7:21).

The lusts of the world include the pride (vainglory) of life. Eve saw the tree was "a tree to be desired to make one wise" (Gen. 3:6). Satan's temptation of Jesus included his questioning, "If thou be the Son of God," appealing to Jesus to tempt (test, try) God by proudly assuming God would save Him (Mat. 4:5-7). The pride of life appeals to the heart of man from which one's actions arise (Pro. 23:7).

THE LOSS OF THE WORLD

(1 John 2:17) The world passes away (is passing away). If one gained everything in the world, he would have lost everything of real worth (Luke 9:25). Unlike the soul of man, the world and the things of it will not last (Mat. 6:19-21). One day, all "things" will pass away (2 Pet. 3:9-11).

The lusts pass away. Not only will the objects of desire pass away, even the desires for the world and its things will not last, but also the punishment for loving them will not pass away. Consider the rich man whose love of the world cost him his soul (Luke 16:19-31). In "torments," his desire certainly was not for good food and fine clothing (Luke 16:19, 25)! Though the world and its lust pass away, the Father, and those who love Him, will abide forever.

We must not love the world, (Jam. 1:27; Rom. 12:2). We must not let love of the world overcome us, but, by faith, overcome it (1 John 5:4). What does it matter? If we love the world and lust after its things, we will lose all these things AND our own souls. If we love the Father, we will abide with Him forever.

MATERIALISM AND OUR TREASURES

> Lay not up for yourselves treasures upon earth, where moth and rust doth corrupt, and where thieves break through and steal: But lay up for yourselves treasures in heaven, where neither moth nor rust doth corrupt, and where thieves do not break through nor steal: For where your treasure is, there will your heart be also. The light of the body is the eye: if therefore thine eye be single, thy whole body shall be full of light. But if thine eye be evil, thy whole body shall be full of darkness. If therefore the light that is in thee be darkness, how great is that darkness! No man can serve two masters: for either he will hate the one, and love the other; or else he will hold to the one, and despise the other. Ye cannot serve God and mammon (Mat. 6:19-24).

Jesus, in this section of the "Sermon on the Mount," presented the choice each man must make, and will make, whether to serve God or mammon. None can serve both at the same time, but each will serve one or the other (v. 24). That which one treasures will determine his choice between the heavenly and the earthly--to be a slave of God, or a slave of mammon (riches). Man chooses what he treasures, and his treasure will have the foremost place in his heart, soul, and mind.

What are treasures? That which one treasures is that which he loves, which he holds in highest regard, and puts in first place in his life, because of the value he places on it, whether in accordance with God-placed values, or in spite of them. Many think of only material wealth as the point of this passage. Truly, such treasure could be possessions of money, wealth, and financial gain of whatever sort; however, included in this context are the other earthly things one might treasure such as popularity, power, position, and pleasure.

We must note that Jesus does not, in this sermon, prohibit one's wise preparation and saving in order to care properly for his family, which care God's Word plainly and strongly enjoins elsewhere, nor is wealth inherently sinful (Mark 10:24; 1 Tim. 6:17).

LAY NOT UP FOR YOURSELVES TREASURES UPON EARTH

(Mat. 6:19). Why lay up treasures that are earthly? These treasures hold the danger of making one poorer for having them, because they can take God's place, and crowd out what is really valuable. They are earth-bound and earth binding, for their earthly possession is the love of the possessor's life. They appeal to the lust of the flesh, the lust of the eye, and the pride of life, and not to the higher, nobler, and purer affections.

Why lay up treasures that are temporary? These are treasures that do not last. At best, they are but temporary, and our days of having them are soon over. At worst, in our brief sojourn, they have us, until we depart this life and leave them all behind.

Why lay up treasures that are subject to loss? Those who trust in such treasures often find out, it is as Jesus said. The moth, in satisfying his appetite, does not consider the worth of his meal, devouring the finest, most expensive garment as readily as a discarded rag. Rust enters the palaces of kings, as it does the hovel of the destitute. Thieves break through (dig through the wall) and steal without regard for the depth of attachment of the former possessor to his treasured belonging. One may be wealthy today and lose it all, ending up a pauper on the morrow, losing not only the things he holds dear in life, but also his reason for living. Why place such value on that which is so fleeting?

LAY UP FOR YOURSELVES TREASURES IN HEAVEN

(Mat. 6:20). Lay up treasures that are heavenly. These treasures are not chosen under the direction of the outward man, but are the choice of the inward man whose faithful continuance leads him to that heavenly home (Col. 3:1-2). One noted that at the close of day, the simple cow does not have to be forced from the far end of the pasture, but waits at the gate, ready to be taken to the barn--for her feed, her treasure is there, and her heart is there. So, the child of God, at the close of his earthly day, is ready to go to where his treasure is, in heaven--where his heart is.

Lay up treasures that are eternal. That which is of real value is not material. It is neither temporary nor transient, but timeless. Why enslave ourselves to mammon, spend our lives seeking its gain, hoarding it greedily, when its possession is so soon to end, and our purpose for living ends with it? That which is of real value is that which is of lasting value.

Lay up treasures that are not subject to loss. Men may lose possessions, physical health, power, popularity, position, and that which brings pleasure, but the treasures that are heavenly will continue. When the faithful servant of God leaves this earth, he leaves behind, as does the servant of mammon, all earthly things, but, unlike mammon's servant, he goes to heaven where he has laid up his riches. No force of nature, man, or the devil himself can remove these treasures from their heavenly store.

FOR WHERE YOUR TREASURE IS, THERE WILL YOUR HEART BE ALSO

(Mat. 6:21). Where are our thoughts? Jesus warned: "Take no thought" for the things of this world. "Take no thought for your life, what ye shall eat, or what ye shall drink; nor yet for your body, what ye shall put on" (Mat. 6:25). "And why take ye thought for raiment?"

(v. 28). "Therefore take no thought, saying, what shall we eat? or, What shall we drink? or, Wherewithal shall we be clothed?" (v. 31). "Take therefore no thought for the morrow" (v. 34). The literal meaning of "take no thought" is "be not anxious"; that is, do not commit the folly of worrying about the earthly, material, temporal things of this world for, "Which of you by taking thought can add one cubit unto his stature?" (v. 27).

Worry is unproductive, burdensome, and, more often than not, in vain. Worry announces one's lack of faith in God and his fear that God will not provide as He has promised. Worry robs one of peace, prevents happiness, presents an improper influence, and hinders his service to God. Where a man's treasure is, there will his thoughts be also.

Where is our trust? In light of Jesus's statement that no man can, at the same time, serve mammon (the god of riches) and God (the God of true riches), in whom do we trust? If our trust is in things, Jesus said we are like the Gentiles (literally, "nations," and, by implication, "heathen," who do not believe in God, "For after all these things do the Gentiles seek" [v.32]), but the same God who has given us our needs has promised to supply our needs. Where a man's treasure is, there will his trust be also.

Where is our treasure? There will be our thoughts, our trust, and our hearts, centered either upon God or mammon! There are only two places where one may lay up treasure--upon earth or in heaven. If our treasure is laid up on earth, these sad conditions must also follow. We have failed to heed God's warning (v. 19). We have failed to follow God's command (v. 20). Our sight is out of focus, and we are in great darkness (vv. 22-23). We are mammon's servants (v. 24). We are too worried about things (v. 25). We have missed the lesson of God's compassionate care (v. 26). We have failed to consider the glory of God's creation (vv. 27-29). We have shown ourselves to be "of little faith" (v. 30). We have behaved as the heathen (vv. 31-32). We have failed to put first things first (v. 33). We have borrowed trouble, worrying about tomorrow, instead of trusting that God can take care of the future (v. 34).

When we consider laying up treasure, there are some important questions that deserve our careful attention. "Is not the life more than meat, and the body than raiment?" (v. 25). The slave of mammon worries about these things. The servant of God is concerned about that which makes life precious, gives us purpose, and offers possibilities of godly service, while the servant of mammon is concerned about things that fill the belly and clothe the body. God's servant sees the value of making a life while mammon's servant can see only the need to make a living. "Are ye not much better than they?" (v. 26). The Father, who made the birds, cares for them, supplying them with food. When was the last time you saw a worried bird? Of how much greater worth are God's children! "Which of you by taking thought can add one cubit to his stature?" (v. 27). One's worry over the measure of his life does not increase it. Being anxious about things will, instead, cause us not to profit in real riches. What a simple lesson, and how we need to learn it! "Wherefore, if God so clothe the grass of the field, which to day is, and to morrow is cast into the oven, shall he not much more clothe you, O ye of little faith?" (v. 30). One of the greatest challenges to man is to trust in God's providential care. Where is our faith? Do we believe God will keep His word to His children?

CONCLUSION

What shall we treasure? The lesson is this: there are some things men must not treasure and there are some things men must treasure. If we treasure the earthly above the heavenly, our prosperity will come to a complete and final end when death comes (if not before). If we treasure the heavenly above the earthly, our reward shall be abundant, heavenly, and eternal.

Remember These Points: Love not the world, nor the things of it. Love the Father. Lay not up for yourselves treasures upon earth. Lay up for yourselves treasures in heaven. The divinely given reason: For where you treasure is, there will your heart be also.

Let us place proper value and priority upon that which is of eternal importance, not upon the things that are earthly, temporary, and material.

STUDY QUESTIONS

1. What is materialism?
2. What are some of the problems of materialism?
3. How prevalent is the problem of materialism?
4. What is the "world" that we are not to love?
5. Why would anyone love the world, and the things of it?
6. What is the meaning of "treasure"?
7. Why not lay up treasures upon the earth?
8. How may one lay up treasures in heaven?
9. Where will our hearts be? Why?
10. When we think of laying up treasure, what questions should we consider?

IMMODEST APPAREL

Stephen Atnip

INTRODUCTION

Christian modesty is a subject often addressed, but many times with a great deal of subjective rather than objective information. Preachers often tread lightly and elderships are often concerned that being too strict will "turn off" those whom we seek to teach. The younger age groups in the church are often told they ought to dress modestly, but the guidelines always seem to be moving with each generation and situation. And some communities, especially like our own here in Florida, are faced with special problems of sun and beaches, where the less you wear, the more acceptable you seem to be. School can also be a minefield for the young saint. In sports, cheerleading is encouraged, with uniforms that reveal quite a bit of the wearer. Even in some sporting events, such as swimming, the attire is nearly non-existent. Running track can involve outfits that expose much of the athlete to the viewer. We are even reminded that ancient athletes used to perform in the nude. Wikipedia, that "bastion of combined ignorance" states, "The wearing of clothing is exclusively a human characteristic and is a feature of most human societies. It is not known when humans began wearing clothes." The Bible is not so historically challenged, informing us that wearing clothes began immediately after the fall in Eden (Gen. 3:21). Thus, there was no evolutionary advancement of man from millions of years of running around in the buff until the present-day fashion consciousness of most civilized nations.

When the Bible is used, usually members of the church feel compelled to use only the New Testament for consideration of modesty. Appeal is often made to 1 Timothy 2:9, "In like manner also, that women adorn themselves in modest apparel…" The word for modest in this passage is from "kosmios" meaning, "well arranged, seemly, modest." Trench adds, "The well ordering is not of dress and demeanour only, but of the inner life; uttering indeed and expressing itself in the outward conversation." Thus, the rest of 1 Timothy 2:9,10 mainly deals with a demeanor of life, rather than a code telling what is too exposing and what is not. The modesty of this passage does include the following thoughts, "not with broided hair, or gold, or pearls, or costly array" (1 Tim. 2:9). This passage has caused some to exclude any kind of jewelry in the assembly. I do not think that this is the meaning of this passage, especially when taken alongside 1 Peter 3:3, 4,

> Whose adorning let it not be that outward adorning of plaiting the hair, and of wearing of gold, or of putting on of apparel; But let it be the hidden man of the heart, in that which is not corruptible, even the ornament of a meek and quiet spirit, which is in the sight of God of great price.

Note again that this is written to Christian wives with unbelieving husbands, whether in the assembly or not in the assembly. Note carefully that the last phrase of verse 3, if taken without using it comparatively with verse 4, would forbid a woman to wear anything. Taken together, it must be obvious that these passages are not forbidding women to wear their golden wedding rings, or other apparel to make themselves presentable. This is rather forbidding an ostentatious display of wealth and opulence that takes the mind off the inner person and centers it on the outward display. In the case of the assembly, such ostentation would be counterproductive to a congregational mind set on God and worship; and in the case of an unbelieving husband, resorting to outward opulence was not the tool to win him to Christ, while a meek and quiet spirit certainly could.

OLD TESTAMENT CONCEPTS

However, we should not limit ourselves to the New Testament in the study of modesty. While it is true that we are living under the New Covenant of Christ, we should keep in mind that the Old Testament still has its profit for us today. Paul wrote to those at Rome, "For whatsoever things were written aforetime were written for our learning, that we through patience and comfort of the scriptures might have hope" (Rom. 15:4). Many of the principles of the Old Testament that deal with a host of matters from family to finance were never part of any covenant system per se, but were simply matters of wisdom that span the ages of time. With that thought in mind, we would notice some of the Old Testament principles that bear on our topic.

THOUGHTS FROM THE GARDEN OF EDEN

When man and woman first lived in the garden, the following statement is made: "And they were both naked, the man and his wife, and were not ashamed" (Gen. 2:25). The concept of being ashamed implies embarrassment and sometimes guilt. Here in our passage the word is from the Hithpael binyan in the Hebrew, expressing reflexive action or causation. There was nothing within the man or the woman which caused them to have the least shame or embarrassment when they were naked.

Now consider their condition after their disobedience in the garden. Moses writes, "And the eyes of them both were opened, and they knew that they were naked; and they sewed fig leaves together, and made themselves aprons" (Gen. 3:7). This statement is worthy of consideration for it tells us at least three things.

First, their eyes were opened. This comes from the Hebrew "nifal binyan," meaning that they were passive in this matter. It happened to them from an external source that entered them and caused their eyes to see things differently. While some people claim the shame associated with nakedness is imposed by society, we would ask, "what society was present in the garden of Eden to have brought on this shame?" This shame came upon our first parents, being imposed on them by what sprang out of the fruit they consumed, and that shame or embarrassment of nakedness has continued for all of mankind through the years that followed. However, mankind is a creature that can be taught out of his natural inclinations. It is not a natural inclination for a mother to kill her unborn child, but she can be persuaded by societal pressure that abortion is a good thing, and thereby act accordingly. Likewise, there is a natural inclination for shame over nakedness in human beings once they grow to the point that their hormones begin to act upon their minds and actions. A newborn has no shame and is like Adam and Eve before the fall; but with age, the natural mind of the child will begin feeling unease and embarrassment when they are unclothed before others.

Second, they knew they were naked. There was a perception of being without covering on their skin. This is not a feeling shared by any other creature in the animal kingdom. No other kind of creature ate the fruit of the knowledge of good and evil. Only man partook, and only man now had a new perception of when he was unclothed. This perception continues to this day only in man.

Third, they felt a need to cover what was embarrassing to them. They chose fig leaves sewed together to cover themselves. The word translated "aprons" in the KJV means "girdles" or "loin cloths." To get an idea of the brevity of these outfits, one need only look at Isaiah 3:24, where it is referred to as a belt-type "sash" (ASV), which was replaced by a rope. The picture is that not very much was made to cover themselves. God later rectifies this situation by clothing them in something other than a loin cloth. He made them coats of animal skins (Gen. 3:21). The Hebrew word for coats means "tunics, a long shirt-like garment." This also shows a feature of Adam and Eve's newfound state that continues to this day. While we are aware of the need for covering, we are not always aware of how we ought to cover ourselves. The American Indian did not go completely without clothing. He wore a loin cloth similar to what we are seeing with Adam and Eve. When Adam and Eve clothed themselves in that fashion, it was insufficient. God stepped in to properly clothe them. People have to be taught how to dress.

Even in the New Testament, the Greek word for "naked" (gumnos) does not mean just naked alone, but also ill clad, or dressed in the undergarment only. After the fall in the garden, Adam and Eve sensed they were bare. They tried to fix it by wearing skimpy outfits. They were ill-clad. When we run around in skimpy revealing garments, we are ill-clad and in need of being clothed. God fixed this situation for Adam and Eve by giving them clothes that covered more than what their brief attire would cover. When we go to the beach or the river today in outfits that cover no more than our present-day underwear covers, we are naked and need to cover ourselves.

Now, no matter what I say, some will still want a better guideline to ascertain what ought to be covered and what may be properly exposed. While it is obvious that God clothed them with a tunic which would have covered at least the middle of the body, there is some question among us as to how high the tunic may have gone, and how low the tunic would have extended to cover the body. As one person said, "Well some cultures think you can't even show your ankles." Then, let us take a further look into the Bible to see if we can find other passages to help us.

COVERING THE LOWER BODY

Look first at Exodus 28:42. This is a passage telling the priests how to dress properly. Even though the priest wore a linen tunic, still, as he approached the altar, the height of the altar, or wind conditions, might create a situation that might cause the priest to expose his nakedness to the people. So we read, "And thou shalt make them linen breeches to cover their nakedness; from the loins even unto the thighs they shall reach." The Hebrew is a phrase which is idiomatic, referring to classes of objects to express the idea of both. In other words, when you expose your loins and thighs, you are exposing your nakedness. The word for thigh is "yarek" referring to the area where the sword was worn and not the Hebrew word "showq" which could include the lower leg calf for men. The Bible is very clear that there ought to be shame on our part when we are exposing our nakedness (Rev. 3:18). Men should take especial reference here to the fact that this is men exposing their thighs. Men, when you expose your thighs, you are exposing your nakedness. If someone should say this is Mosaic a law, I would point out to them the law did not make men naked. This Mosaic law only told them how to cover nakedness by wearing linen pants to cover their loins and thighs. The fact of what is naked has nothing to do with any law. The law simply told them how to cover it. Whatever method I choose to cover my nakedness today is up to me, but I need to cover it. Thus, if I show my calves or ankles, I am not showing nakedness.

Now, ladies, this same principle of nakedness is applied to you,

> Take the millstones, and grind meal: uncover thy locks, make bare the leg, uncover the thigh, pass over the rivers. Thy nakedness shall be uncovered, yea, thy shame shall be seen, Isaiah 47:2,3.

This is the picture of Babylon going into destruction under the figure of a woman coming to a river to cross over. She uncovers her thighs after removing the flowing skirt. God says this is uncovering her nakedness. Ladies, when many women go to the beach today, and get ready to step into the water, most do not bother to even wear the flowing skirt. They just walk around exposing their thighs with no covering whatsoever. This is nakedness according to the Bible's definition.

COVERING THE UPPER BODY

What about the upper part of the body? For the woman there is a consideration unique to her gender. The writer of Proverbs 5:18,19 states, "rejoice with the wife of thy youth. 19 Let her be as the loving hind and pleasant roe; let her breasts satisfy thee at all times; and be thou ravished always with her love." The word for satisfied is the Hebrew word "rava" in the piel binyan, meaning to be "drunk, intoxicated, saturated, figuratively to sate." The idea is one of sexually filling the senses. A woman should always understand this aspect of a man's make-up. This part of her body is to be reserved for her husband in their intimate relationship with one another. The stipulation in Proverbs is to the husband to keep his mind on his wife and her charms, rather than on what another woman may expose to him. The implication here is rather clear. A woman's breasts should be kept covered to any but her husband, who is to delight in her alone. When a woman exposes her breasts or cleavage to other men, she needs to know it has an impact on the male gender. This is by God's design such impact should be made, but only between a husband and wife. When a woman purposely exposes herself in public, she is immodest and imposing a hardship on the opposite gender which is ungodly. Her breasts are for satisfying and filling the senses of her husband alone.

THE PROBLEM WITH THE FLESH

Allow me for a moment to point out a reality that is often either not known or else is misunderstood. Sometimes a woman will expose herself and when men look at her, she will say, "That is his problem," or "He is just a dirty old man." I wonder why they do not say, "He is a just dirty young man?" Paul points out in Romans 7:15-19, 23-24,

> For that which I do I allow not: for what I would, that do I not; but what I hate, that do I. If then I do that

> which I would not, I consent unto the law that it is good. Now then it is no more I that do it, but sin that dwelleth in me. For I know that in me (that is, in my flesh,) dwelleth no good thing: for to will is present with me; but how to perform that which is good I find not. For the good that I would I do not: but the evil which I would not, that I do.... But I see another law in my members, warring against the law of my mind, and bringing me into captivity to the law of sin which is in my members. O wretched man that I am! who shall deliver me from the body of this death?

You see, at a certain stage of development, the human body begins to receive a surge of hormonally induced passions and desires. They are not active in the newborn, or the small child. But around the age of puberty, these hormones are released into our bodies and there are passions that react, as in the animal kingdom. They do not regulate themselves. They simply are present in the body and the spiritual man must regulate these passions. Romans 8:7 points out, this carnal or fleshly mind, or set of impulses is not subject to the law of God, neither indeed can it be. That simply means when you get hungry, you cannot read thirty verses and expect the appetite to go away. Neither is it the case when you have hormonal impulses, just because the Bible forbids a certain wrong action, that does not mean your body's passions will quit wanting to see wrong, hear wrong or do wrong. As long as you are in the flesh, your body's hormones will continue to press you to obey their will. The body is made to respond to sexual stimuli, and all the Bible reading in the world will not stop the body from naturally reacting to such stimuli. The thing that makes you different from the birds and bees is the fact human beings also have a spiritual man that is subject to the law of God; you have to use your spiritual man to regulate your body's hormonal impulses. It is not at all easy at times. Therefore, Paul says it is a constant warring between you and your fleshly desires, and exclaims at the end, "Oh wretched man that I am, who shall deliver me from this body which is intent on having its way, even at the cost of the death of my soul?"

Now, men and women, listen carefully. If you expose these areas of your body that are naked, and are reserved for intimate satisfaction between a husband and wife alone, you place an incredible battle of the mind upon the opposite gender. They are not dirty old men or women, when you expose what naturally excites and arouses the sexual elements of the mind. That response is as natural as a new-born babe with a rooting instinct to suckle at its mother's breast. The advertising world is well aware of this natural phenomenon. That is why they post pictures of women and men exposing their nakedness on billboards. The more they expose on the sign, they realize the inner man of the flesh is drawn to the sign by natural instinct. This is also true in stores. If you want to get someone to look at your product, just show the nakedness of a man or woman on the sign.

The person (other than your mate) whose gaze you attract with your exposure of your body in immodesty does indeed sin, if they allow that exposure to cause them to lust after you. But when you expose yourself in such a fashion, remember the first "dirty" person is YOU, when you willfully excite the natural impulses of the opposite gender without regard for what is totally natural within them. You can say whatever you wish to justify your own ungodly behavior, but remember this, your final judge is God and He has already told you how to cover yourself.

Now the world will hear what I have said, and call it every name in the book, but they know it to be true. At the Clay County courthouse where prisoners are kept, there is a dress code on the wall for visitors. It wasn't written by preachers. It was set there by people who saw the results of nakedness on prisoners. That dress code requires the covering of those areas we have seen talked about in the Bible. Call it Purtanical, Victorian, prudish, male chauvinism, or any other name you wish to call it. The bottom line is that it is reality, and Christians should seek to follow God in their lives.

OTHER CONSIDERATIONS

But what about the fact I have to live in a world that exposes its nakedness without regard to the Bible's teaching? Let me offer some quick considerations:

First, young people, I know those at school who expose themselves get attention, but it is the wrong attention. And the person who is attracted to one person exposing themselves on Monday, will set eyes on the next one who exposes more of themselves on Tuesday. Do you really wish to have the father or mother of your children be a person whose care for you relies only on what they see of your body? A relationship built predominantly on hormones cannot pass the tests of time, and the years that follow can be very lonely, povertous and spiritually bankrupt, as your fleshly mate falls for anything that will expose itself to him or her. Young people, do not let the world press you into its mold (Rom. 12:2); and it certainly will if you let it. Follow God's word. It will give you the relationship of love and intimacy God reserves only for His children.

Second, learn to turn you eyes away from that which excites passion. Job said in the long ago, "I made a covenant with mine eyes; why then should I think upon a maid?" (Job 31:1). It is one thing to see someone in my daily world of the office or school, or to see some advertisement on a billboard, that comes up on the side of the road, or in the newspaper, or in a magazine. It is one thing to have it sneak up on me, but something altogether different when I linger to look. Make a covenant with your eyes to turn away when you see something you know will naturally excite you when you have no right to enjoy its pleasures. Further, do not go hunting a view of the nakedness of the flesh, whether it be in the movies, porn on the internet, my sunbathing neighbor, the views at the beach, or any other place where people expose their nakedness without any regard for what it does to others.

CONCLUSION

Christian modesty is not as subjective a topic as many people believe. It is a topic certainly covered by the Bible. We have not exhausted all the concepts of the Bible with regard to Christian modesty, but we ought to at least put these principles into practice in our lives and have respect for the great warfare our Christian brothers and sisters have to fight in their struggle for eternal life. Remember while this lesson predominantly covered the proper understanding of nakedness and the shame that ought to be associated with it, there is also a second consideration of the proper clothing of the spiritual man as we noted in 1 Peter 3:1-4. When physical modesty is coupled with spiritual adornment, a person will never find a better best friend or mate.

STUDY QUESTIONS

1. Why is Christian modesty such a difficult subject today?
2. What passages in the New Testament are often used to talk about modesty, and how do they impact our subject of modesty?
3. Why should we not remove the Old Testament as a help in the area of Christian modesty?
4. What caused Adam and Eve to sense their own nakedness?
5. How does the Bible show the thigh as an area men should cover up?
6. How does the Bible show the thigh as an area for women to cover up?
7. What does the Bible's teaching in Proverbs 5:18, 19 teach a woman about her dress and its impact on the male mind?
8. Discuss the natural instincts of men and women as it relates to their reactions to immodesty.
9. What are some things that Christian men and women should consider as they dress themselves?
10. What are some things we can do to help to control our natural instincts in a world that dresses immodestly?

ENDNOTES

1. History of Nudity - Wikipedia, the Free Encyclopedia," n.d. http://en.wikipedia.org/wiki/History_of_nudity.

   Ibid.

2. Thayer, Joseph H., ed. Thayer's Greek-English Lexicon of the New Testament: Being Grimm's Wilke's Clavis Novi Testamenti: Numerically Coded to Strong's Exhaustive Concordance. Grand Rapids, Michigan: Baker Academic, 1977.

3. Trench, Richard C. Synonyms of the New Testament. Nnth ed. Grand Rapids, Michigan: William B. Eerdman's Publishing Company, 1880.

4. Guralnik, David B., ed. "Ashamed." Webster's New World Dictionary of the American Language. Simon and Schuster, 1982.

5. Weingreen, J. A Practical Grammar For Classical Hebrew Second Edition. 2d ed. Oxford, 1972.

6. Brown, Francis, S. R. Driver, and Charles A. Briggs. Brown-Driver-Briggs Hebrew and English Lexicon. Complete and Unabridged, fully searchable, with Strong Numbers and interactive Index. Hendrickson Pub, 1996.

7. Ibid

8. Thayer, Thayer's Greek-English Lexicon of the New Testament, 122.

9. Brown, Driver, and Briggs, Brown-Driver-Briggs Hebrew, and English Lexicon, 724.

10. Ibid., 1003

11. Ibid., 724

AUTHORITY IN MORALITY

Melvin Sapp

INTRODUCTION

We live in a time where morals are no longer stationary or fixed, but they are fluctuating and changing all the time. Society is no longer clear on what is right and what is wrong morally. The lines are being blurred and definitions are being changed. Evil is being called good and good is being called evil. Every new generation is pushing for the acceptance of looser morals and appealing to weaker standards in determining what is morally acceptable. The Christian needs to be aware of the human philosophies that encourage immorality, and he must be knowledgeable about true standards of authorities in morality.

The word "authority" is translated from the Greek word 'exousia' and is defined by W.E. Vine as "possessing the right to exercise power; or being given the right to command obedience." Thus, for there to be a moral standard, someone must possess the authority to set the boundaries for what constitute morality.

The word "morality" is defined as a system of moral conduct, particular moral principles or rules of conduct regulating human activity, a system that determines whether human conduct is right or wrong. The things that are right are moral and the things that are wrong are immoral. Who or what determines what is right and what is wrong as it relates to human conduct?

FALSE AUTHORITIES MASQUERADING AS MORAL STANDARDS ATHEISM

Atheism is a human philosophy that denies and rejects the existence of God. Our education system has accepted atheism as fact and has indoctrinated our young people with this faith-destroying philosophy. Worldly wisdom has rejected the evidence of the Creator to their own shame and corruption.

> Because that which may be known of God is manifest in them; for God hath shewed it unto them. For the invisible things of him from the creation of the world are clearly seen, being understood by the things that are made, even his eternal power and Godhead; so that they are without excuse: Because that, when they knew God, they glorified him not as God, neither were thankful; but became vain in their imaginations, and their foolish heart was darkened. Professing themselves to be wise, they became fools, And changed the glory of the uncorruptible God into an image made like to corruptible man, and to birds, and fourfooted beasts, and creeping things. Wherefore God also gave them up to uncleanness through the lusts of their own hearts, to dishonour their own bodies between themselves: Who changed the truth of God into a lie, and worshipped and served the creature more than the Creator, who is blessed for ever. Amen (Rom. 1:19-25).

Atheists affirm that they "know" God does not exist. Scientific knowledge is gained through investigation using the empirical senses. God is spirit and cannot be seen, heard, felt, smelled nor tasted. It is, therefore, outside of science to prove or to disprove the existence of God. Such statements show their conclusions are bias and are drawn on emotions and not on evidence. The Psalmist wrote: "the fool hath said in his heart, there is no God. They are corrupt, they have done abominable works, there is none that doeth good" (Psa. 14:1). To make judgments without respecting the abundance evidence is indeed foolish!

What makes atheism so appealing to the elite of society? If God can be removed from His universe, then there would be no supreme Judge, Judgment Day, Heaven nor Hell to face after this life. Psalm 7:11 teaches, "God judgeth the righteous, and God is angry with the wicked every day." The thought of being judged by a perfect and all-knowing God is terrifying to the ungodly. God is real and He will be the judge of all men. "To the general assembly and church of the firstborn, which are written in heaven, and to God the Judge of all, and to the spirits of just men made perfect" (Heb. 12:23). The Bible assures us that every person will be judged according to how we have lived. "For we must all appear before the judgment seat of Christ; that every one may receive the things done in his body, according to that he hath done, whether it be good or bad" (2 Cor. 5:10). Atheists want to run God out of His universe to remove themselves for being judged for the way that they live. Yet, "...let God be true, but every man a liar…" (Rom. 3:4).

Evolution

Evolution is another pillar of humanism that teaches the world came into existence by chance and not by intelligent design Again, the Bible affirms in Hebrews 11:3; "Through faith we understand that the worlds were framed by the word of God, so that things which are seen were not made of things which do appear." Faith is produced by the evidence that the Bible is God's inspired revelation. "So then faith cometh by hearing, and hearing by the word of God" (Rom. 10:17). Evolution believes everything that exists came from nothing.

Evolution believes life evolved from non-living matter and has become more complex over eons of time. Man is believed to be the end of the evolutionary chain, having survived countless mutations. The Bible reveals the origin of man as being the crown of God's creation.

> And God said, Let us make man in our image, after our likeness: and let them have dominion over the fish of the sea, and over the fowl of the air, and over the cattle, and over all the earth, and over every creeping thing that creepeth upon the earth. So God created man in his own image, in the image of God created he him; male and female created he them (Gen. 1:26-27).

Either the world was created by intelligent designer or it came into existence by chance. Even science believes in the law of causation or Cause and Effect, that every effect has an equal or adequate cause. The existence of the world demands that something caused it to come into existence (Heb. 3:4). "For every house is builded by some man; but he that built all things is God." The presence of a house demands that somebody built it! It would be illogical to conclude that a house built itself or it just happened by chance.

Evolution devalues man to the level of an animal in teaching that he evolved from lower life forms. The sophistication of man's physical body with all its systems makes it incomprehensible to conclude that those systems just happened over eons of time. If man is just an animal, then he does not possess a soul and is no better than a cow. "For what is a man profited, if he shall gain the whole world, and lose his own soul? or what shall a man give in exchange for his soul?" (Matt. 16:26). If the evolutionists accepts that man has a soul, he must also accept he did not get it from a monkey. Evolution is a godless philosophy that elevates man and denies God.

Values Clarification

Humanism seeks to legislate what is moral and what is immoral by redefining morals under the cloak of "Values Clarification." Moral clarification is an attempt to make immorality acceptable by changing the names to more acceptable designations. Calling certain activities sinful or immoral carries a guilt trip that discourages that activity by making it taboo.

Fornication is called safe sex. "Shacking up" is called a committed relationship. Drinking alcohol is called "socializing." Drug use is called "experimenting." Profanity is called "adult language." Homosexuality is called "alternate lifestyle."

Reclassification of values seeks to remove guilt to make sin palatable. Those who refuse to accept these reclassifications are ridiculed and labeled as old-fashioned, narrow-minded, and hateful. Sanitizing sin and calling it by another name does not change it from being sin. It is not the name that makes sin immoral, but the activity itself.

Situation Ethics

Situation ethics is a worldly philosophy that makes personal feelings the standard in determining right from wrong. If it feels good to you, do it! There is no higher power or standard than one's own belief. The situation determines what is right and what is wrong. There is no objective standard for every person. Every person becomes his own standard. If it brings you pleasure and satisfaction then it is right, but if it brings pain and unhappiness, then it is to be avoided. Wrong is not wrong if it feels good. Wrong is not wrong if it is popular. Wrong is not wrong if you do not get caught. Wrong is not wrong if some good comes out of it.

Situation ethics rejects the Bible as God's authorized objective, standard and elevates man's subjective feelings as his standard. This damnable philosophy encourages sin and denigrates man into an immoral beast.

Self Autonomy

Self autonomy is another pillar of humanism that makes man only responsible to himself. If you reject the existence of God, the authenticity of the Bible and a future Day of Judgment, then man is only answerable to himself. If there is not a universal standard applicable to all men, then it does not matter whether your action are good nor bad. Laws and rules only regulate social relationships but are not binding as one is free to govern himself.

The Bible is rejected as inspired or authoritative and man is left with his personal feelings and judgments. The Bible denounces man's ability to govern himself. "O LORD, I know that the way of man is not in himself: it is not in man that walketh to direct his steps" (Jer. 10:23). "There is a way which seemeth right unto a man, but the end thereof are the ways of death" (Prov. 14:12).

These are some of the false authorities that are prominent in lowering the morals of our nation and making immorality socially acceptable.

TRUE AUTHORITIES IN MORALITY

There are true and objective standards in morality that need to be respected. We need to be open to investigate the evidence for divine objective standards in morality.

God has all authority

There is a God in Heaven who is all-wise, eternal, and all-powerful. "The heavens declare the glory of God; and the firmament sheweth his handywork" (Psa. 19:1). There is an abundance of empirical evidence all around us that proves the existence of God. The orderly arrangement of our universe could not have happened by chance, but by intelligent design.

God created the world and man with such sophistication that it is undeniable that their existence must be attributed to God. Being that God is creator, it is immoral to reject His authority over His creation. "For the invisible things of him from the creation of the world are clearly seen, being understood by the things that are made, even his eternal power and Godhead; so that they are without excuse" (Rom. 1:20). God holds man accountable for the way he lives and will judge him accordingly. Romans 14:11-12 states; "For it is written, As I live, saith the Lord, every knee shall bow to me, and every tongue shall confess to God. So then every one of us shall give account of himself to God." Rejecting God is not going to remove Him as judge nor cancel our appointment to come before Him.

Jesus has been delegated all authority

Jesus existed in eternity with God as the Word and came to save man from his sins. "In the beginning was the Word, and the Word was with God, and the Word was God. The same was in the beginning with God. All things were made by him; and without him was not any thing made that was made" (Jn. 1:1-3). Jesus paid the price to be Savior by accepting the humiliation of death.

> Let this mind be in you, which was also in Christ Jesus: Who, being in the form of God, thought it not robbery to be equal with God: But made himself of no reputation, and took upon him the form of a servant, and was made in the likeness of men: And being found in fashion as a man, he humbled himself, and became obedient unto death, even the death of the cross. Wherefore God also hath highly exalted him, and given him a name which is above every name: That at the name of Jesus every knee should bow, of things in heaven, and things in earth, and things under the earth; And that every tongue should confess that Jesus Christ is Lord, to the glory of God the Father (Phil. 2:5-11).

Jesus is in such an elevated position that every person is under His authority. No one can get to heaven except they come through Jesus. Every person will confess Jesus either by choice in this life or by compulsion at the Day of Judgment.

Jesus has been given all authority in religious matters today.

> And Jesus came and spake unto them, saying, All power is given unto me in heaven and in earth. Go ye therefore, and teach all nations, baptizing them in the name of the Father, and of the Son, and of the Holy Ghost: Teaching them to observe all things whatsoever I have commanded you: and, lo, I am with you alway, even unto the end of the world. Amen (Matt. 28:18-20).

The New Testament is Jesus' legislation on religion and morality. Jesus teaches that fornication is sin and is the only ground for a divorce and remarriage (Matt. 19:9). "And I say unto you, Whosoever shall put away his wife, except it be for fornication, and shall marry another, committeth adultery: and whoso marrieth her which is put away doth commit adultery." Legislators have written laws that allow divorce for many causes other than fornication, but their authority is not above the authority of Christ. Jesus does not change His divine legislation to accommodate the popular divorce laws of our land. "Marriage is honourable in all, and the bed undefiled: but whoremongers and adulterers God will judge" (Heb. 13:4). "There is one lawgiver, who is able to save and to destroy: who art thou that judgest another" (Jas. 4:12).

Jesus also confines marriage between a male and a female. "And he answered and said unto them, Have ye not read, that he which made them at the beginning made them male and female, And said, For this cause shall a man leave father and mother, and shall cleave to his wife: and they twain shall be one flesh" (Matt. 19:4-5). God only made two sexes--male and female. Only males marrying females qualify to marry with God's approval. Only males marrying females can reproduce and perpetuate the human race. Homosexual relationships and marriages are immoral and are unnatural. They are not alternative lifestyles but sinful lifestyles that will keep people out of heaven.

Jesus is Lord of all and will be the Judge of all men. Neither society nor civil rulers are the authority in morality. Jesus will be the final judge of all men and He will judge according to righteousness (Acts 17:30-31). "And the times of this ignorance God winked at; but now commandeth all men every where to repent: Because he hath appointed a day, in the which he will judge the world in righteousness by that man whom he hath ordained; whereof he hath given assurance unto all men, in that he hath raised him from the dead."

The Scriptures have all authority

The Scriptures are inspired of God and regulates all men living today. "All scripture is given by inspiration of God, and is profitable for doctrine, for reproof, for correction, for instruction in righteousness: That the man of God may be perfect, throughly furnished unto all good works" (2 Tim. 3:16-17). Every person who is willing to submit to God will submit to the Scriptures. The Scriptures are given to instruct us into living righteously. Thus, the Scriptures are our authority in determining what is right in regard to morals.

The New Testament has binding authority on every person living today. Some believe the Bible is only binding on those who accept it, or are willing to submit unto it. However, the Scriptures are binding on every person living today.

The Scriptures determine right from wrong for all people in both religion and in morals. God regulates those who refuse to obey the gospel and will punish them for their defiance.

> And to you who are troubled rest with us, when the Lord Jesus shall be revealed from heaven with his mighty angels, In flaming fire taking vengeance on them that know not God, and that obey not the gospel of our Lord Jesus Christ: Who shall be punished with everlasting destruction from the presence of the Lord, and from the glory of his power (2 Thess. 1:7-9).

Our morals will be judged by the Word of God whether we live morally or immorally.

> And I saw the dead, small, and great, stand before God; and the books were opened: and another book was opened, which is the book of life: and the dead were judged out of those things which were written in the books, according to their works. And the sea gave up the dead which were in it; and death and hell delivered up the dead which were in them: and they were judged every man according to their works. And death and hell were cast into the lake of fire. This is the second death. And whosoever was not found written in the book of life was cast into the lake of fire (Rev. 20:12-15).

Positives in Morality

We are to love God and keep His commandments (Matt. 22:36-38). "Master, which is the great commandment in the law? Jesus said unto him, Thou shalt love the Lord thy God with all thy heart, and with all thy soul, and with all thy mind. This is the first and great commandment." Every person is to strive to have the right attitude toward the God of heaven. We are also to love your neighbor as yourself (Matt. 22:39).

We are taught to do unto others as you would have them do unto you (Matt. 7:12). "Therefore all things whatsoever ye would that men should do to you, do ye even so to them: for this is the law and the prophets." It matters how we treat other people, because it determines how we will be treated!

The Bible is plain that sex in marriage is honorable. "Marriage is honourable in all, and the bed undefiled: but whoremongers and adulterers God will judge" (Heb. 13:4). To avoid abusing sex and turning that which is moral into immorality, get married. "Now concerning the things whereof ye wrote unto me: It is good for a man not to touch a woman. Nevertheless, to avoid fornication, let every man have his own wife, and let every woman have her own husband" (1 Cor. 7:1-2). When we fulfill our appetites according to God's design, it is moral. When we fulfill our appetites according to Satan's perversions, it becomes immorality.

Negatives in Morality

Pornography is sin in the heart that seeks sexual pleasure in an illicit way (Matt. 5:27-28). "Ye have heard that it was said by them of old time, Thou shalt not commit adultery: But I say unto you, That whosoever looketh on a woman to lust after her hath committed adultery with her already in his heart." The heart has to be protected against immorality or it will become desperately wicked. "The heart is deceitful above all things, and desperately wicked: who can know it" (Jer. 17:9)?

Abortion on demand kills innocent babies under the banner of "choice." God hates the shedding of innocent blood and abortion is responsible for the shedding of millions of babies' blood. "These six things doth the LORD hate: yea, seven are an abomination unto him: A proud look, a lying tongue, and hands that shed innocent blood" (Prov. 6:16-17). The souls of aborted babes will cry out at the Day of Judgment for justice.

> And when he had opened the fifth seal, I saw under the altar the souls of them that were slain for the word of God, and for the testimony which they held: And they cried with a loud voice, saying, How long, O Lord,

> holy and true, dost thou not judge and avenge our blood on them that dwell on the earth? And white robes were given unto every one of them; and it was said unto them, that they should rest yet for a little season, until their fellowservants also and their brethren, that should be killed as they were, should be fulfilled (Rev. 6:9-11).

Gambling is a violation of fair compensation for honest work. "Let him that stole steal no more: but rather let him labour, working with his hands the thing which is good, that he may have to give to him that needeth" (Eph. 4:28).

All forms of immorality will keep people out of heaven.

> Know ye not that the unrighteous shall not inherit the kingdom of God? Be not deceived: neither fornicators, nor idolaters, nor adulterers, nor effeminate, nor abusers of themselves with mankind, Nor thieves, nor covetous, nor drunkards, nor revilers, nor extortioners, shall inherit the kingdom of God. And such were some of you: but ye are washed, but ye are sanctified, but ye are justified in the name of the Lord Jesus, and by the Spirit of our God (1 Cor. 6:9-11)

CONCLUSION

There are many false authorities that people listen to when it comes to what is moral and what is immoral. False standards mislead people into a false sense of security when in reality they are living in rebellion to God. It is our responsibility to warn and teach people God's standards of morality so to help people get to heaven. May we never be blinded by false standards of authority, but ever respect the truth that is revealed in God's Word about what is right and what is wrong. "...let God be true, but every man a liar…" (Rom. 3:4).

STUDY QUESTIONS

1. Define the word "authority?"
2. Define the word "morality?"
3. What makes atheism so appealing to the elite of society?
4. What is the law of causation?
5. Explain what "Value Clarification" seeks to accomplish in society?
6. What worldly philosophy makes personal feelings the standard in determining right from wrong?
7. Define "Self Autonomy?"
8. What relationship does God have to man that justifies God determining what is moral?
9. What passage emphasizes that Jesus has all authority over all nations in religion and morality?

   What passage teaches that the Scriptures are given to instruct us in living righteously?

LYING AND CORRUPT COMMUNICATION

Bobby Liddell

INTRODUCTION

God hates lying.

> These six things doth the LORD hate: yea, seven are an abomination unto him: A proud look, a lying tongue, and hands that shed innocent blood, An heart that deviseth wicked imaginations, feet that be swift in running to mischief, A false witness that speaketh lies, and he that soweth discord among brethren (Pro. 6:16-19).

God is the "God of truth" (Deu. 32:4), and cannot lie (John 14:6; Tit. 1:2; Heb. 6:18; Num. 23:19; 1 Sam. 15:29; Psa. 89:35); thus, His Word is Truth (John 17:17). God has decreed that "all liars, shall have their part in the lake which burneth with fire and brimstone: which is the second death" (Rev. 21:8). Surely, we can understand the need to repent of all lying in the past, cease from all lying in the present, and abstain from the sin of lying in the future (Col. 3:9). To do this, we need instruction and encouragement from the Word of God, and a consistent practice of telling the truth.

The problem of corrupt communication is a second facet of our study and goes hand-in-hand with the study of lying. Both are sins of the tongue. Hear God's Word on the matter: "Let no corrupt communication proceed out of your mouth, but that which is good to the use of edifying, that it may minister grace unto the hearers" (Eph. 4:29). Corrupt means that which is rotten, but God's people have put away such speech, and seek to speak only that which is good, pure, and wholesome.

THE SIN OF LYING AND CORRUPT COMMUNICATION

The sin of lying. Lying dates back to the serpent's sinful subterfuge in the Garden of Eden, the first sin upon earth, when Satan lied--and accused God of being the liar (Gen. 3:4-5; cf. John 8:44)! Throughout history, "Lying has ever been one of the common, if not one of the commonest, vices of the race."[1] However, truth goes all the way back to eternity, for God, who is truth, and the source of truth, is eternal (Deu. 33:27; 1 Tim. 1:17; Heb. 9:14). Those who lie are of the devil and behave as his children. "When is a man more like Satan, than when he is lying?"[2] Of the devil, Jesus said, "He was a murderer from the beginning, and abode not in the truth, because there is no truth in him. When he speaketh a lie, he speaketh of his own: for he is a liar, and the father of it" (John 8:44). Oliver Wendell Holmes fittingly portrayed sin's dependence upon lying deception: "Sin has many tools, but a lie is the handle which fits them all."[3] The Hebrews writer penned: "But exhort one another daily, while it is called To day; lest any of you be hardened through the deceitfulness of sin" (Heb. 3:13). Indeed, sin is deceptive, promising everything, but delivering only sorrow, separation, and doom. Sin's attraction is a lie. As did Pilate, many ask, "What is truth?" (John 18:38). According to one survey, 67% of Americans do not believe in absolute truth.[4] Citing the book, The Day America Told The Truth, 91% of us lie regularly, most cannot go a week without lying, and 20% cannot get through a day without lying.[5] Men often prefer lies: "Thou lovest evil more than good; and lying rather than to speak righteousness" (Psa. 52:3). Many, like the Jews Jesus addressed, will believe a lie when they will not believe the truth: "And because I tell you the truth, ye believe me not" (John 8:45). Such men will "trust in lying words, that cannot profit" (Jer. 7:8), and "be damned who believed not the truth, but had pleasure in unrighteousness" (2 The. 2:12). Micah correctly set forth the preference of the people for lying prophets (Mic. 2:11). True prophets of God sounded His warning concerning lying prophets who, God said, "prophesy a lie in my name" (Jer. 27:15, 10, 14, 16; 28:15; 29:21, 31; Eze. 21:29; 22:28; Zec. 10:2). Often, the people listened to the lying prophets, for, as Jeremiah recorded, "my people love to have it so" (Jer. 5:31). As is all sin, so all lies are against God (Acts 5:3-4). The "father of lies" entered Paradise on earth, but God will not allow liars in His eternal Paradise (Rev. 21:27; 22:15).

B. C. Goodpasture wrote: "We cannot conform truth to ourselves, but we can conform ourselves to truth."[6] For a sad example of "situation ethics," and "relative truth," consider the following. The Catholic Encyclopedia states: "So that a false statement knowingly made to one who has not a right to the truth will not be a lie,"[7] and, "However we are also under an obligation to keep secrets faithfully, and sometimes the easiest way of fulfilling that duty is to say what is false, or to tell a lie."[8] Again, "A Catholic who on being asked denies that he is one, does not necessarily deny the faith. Such an answer might merely be a fitting reply to an impertinent question."[9] Thomas Aquinas, wrote in Summa Theologica, "Now it is evident that the greater the good intended, the more is the sin of lying diminished in gravity."[10] How different was the perception of Theodore Roosevelt, who said:

> "Liar" is just as ugly a word as "thief," because it implies the presence of just as ugly a sin in one case as in the other....We need fearless criticism of dishonest men, and of honest men on any point where they go wrong; but even more do we need criticism which shall be truthful both in what it says and in what it leaves unsaid--truthful in words and truthful in the impression it designs to leave upon the readers' or hearers' minds. [11]

"No lie is of the truth" (1 John 2:21), whether conveyed by a direct statement, false witness, breaking a vow, leaving a false impression, talebearing/gossip, slander, telling a "partial truth," exaggeration, hypocrisy, flattery, or by silence (Gen. 20:2; Psa. 101:5; 12:2; Pro. 10:18; Eph. 4:25; 2 Pet. 2:18; et al.). Truthfulness is a foundational element of a free society. As Representative Henry J. Hyde, in his statement at the Judiciary Committee hearing on December 2, 1998, so succinctly stated, "Lying poisons justice. If we are to defend justice and the rule of law, lying must have consequences."[12] If we place no premium upon truth, and no penalty upon lying, we remove the underpinning upon which our homes, businesses, governments, and churches rely. In every aspect of civilized society, there must be grounds for trust, or it all falls down. In such a situation, the wicked rule, and the righteous weep. God, through Ezekiel, denounced liars of his day, "Because with lies ye have made the heart of the righteous sad, whom I have not made sad; and strengthened the hands of the wicked, that he should not return from his wicked way, by promising him life" (Eze. 13:22).

In view of the above, why do men lie? First, it is a heart problem. "For out of the heart proceed evil thoughts, murders, adulteries, fornications, thefts, false witness, blasphemies: These are the things which defile a man" (Mat. 15:19-20). Some lies are made in an effort to please another, to avoid offending someone, to boast, or in jest. Some lie to hurt another. Potiphar's wife falsely charged the pure and godly Joseph because he had spurned her advances (Gen. 39:14). "A lying tongue hateth those that are afflicted by it; and a flattering mouth worketh ruin" (Pro. 26:28).

Some lie to save their pride or position. Aaron said, when confronted with the sin of making the idol, the golden calf, "So they gave it (the gold, BL) me: then I cast it into the fire, and there came out this calf" (Exo. 32:24).

Some lie for advantage, to deceive for gain. Gehazi, Elisha's servant, lied to Naaman to receive two talents of silver and two changes of garments, and received leprosy as well (2 Kin. 5:15-27). "The getting of treasures by a lying tongue is a vanity tossed to and fro of them that seek death" (Pro. 21:6).

Some lies are set forth in an effort to protect themselves, to avoid detection and punishment, or upon being caught, to shift blame. After sinning, Adam tried to blame Eve--and God (Gen. 3:12)! Eve, unable to hide, pointed the finger of blame at the serpent (Gen. 3:13). When Peter was identified as one who had been with Jesus, "he began to curse and to swear, saying, I know not this man of whom ye speak" (Mark 14:71).

Some lie to promote their positions in religion. The Jewish rulers, fearful of losing their power and popularity to Jesus, sought false witnesses to accuse Him (Mat. 26:59-ff). Because some will "not endure sound doctrine...after their own lusts shall they heap to themselves teachers, having itching ears" (2 Tim. 4:3). As long as some will listen to the fables of men, there will be men who will supply them (2 Tim. 4:4).

The sin of corrupt communication. Note these warnings from God's Word. "Either make the tree good, and his fruit good; or else make the tree corrupt, and his fruit corrupt: for the tree is known by his fruit" (Mat. 12:33; cf. Luke 6:43). "But now ye also put off all these; anger, wrath, malice, blasphemy, filthy communication out of your mouth" (Col. 3:8). "Let no corrupt communication proceed out of your mouth, but that which is good to the use of edifying, that it may minister grace unto the hearers" (Eph. 4:29). "But fornication, and all uncleanness, or covetousness, let it not be once named among you, as becometh saints; Neither filthiness, nor foolish talking, nor jesting, which are not convenient: but rather giving of thanks" (Eph. 5:3-4). "Thou shalt not take the name of the Lord thy God in vain; for the Lord will not hold him guiltless that taketh his name in vain" (Exo. 20:7). "But above all things, my brethren, swear not, neither by heaven, neither by the earth, neither by any other oath: but let your yea be yea; and your nay, nay; lest ye fall into condemnation" (Jam. 5:12).

How ironic that with the tongue, we may praise God, proclaim the Gospel, and promote good, and with the tongue, we may also swear, curse, and take God's name in vain. We can sweeten our lips with pure, sweet words, or we can spiel forth with filth and rottenness. "Out of the same mouth proceedeth blessing and cursing. My brethren, these things ought not so to be" (Jam. 3:10). Our tongues can be used for good or evil, and we make the choice. We can choose to control our tongues, but we can never allow our tongues to run loose (Jam. 3:8).

What is corrupt communication? It is described by and includes profanity, irreverence in speech, immoral, lewd, lascivious, improper words, suggestive innuendo, and indecent, obscene, offensive, abusive, shameful, ungodly, or unbecoming talk. It is speech that denigrates, debases, defiles, and destroys. In our society, there is little, or no shame attached to corrupt communication. Even some church members tell off-color jokes, and use euphemisms, and "mild" curse words. Why is there such a problem?

There is a lack of control of the mind. "For as he thinketh in his heart, so is he" (Pro. 23:7). Corrupt words come from corrupt minds (1 Tim. 6:5; 2 Tim. 3:8). We will never control our lips until we control our minds.

There is a lack of sufficient vocabulary, or of ability to place emphasis correctly. The interjectory curse word is considered by some to be the ultimate underline, and the extreme exclamation point. Some use "bad words" as an excuse for not training themselves to communicate effectively so they can express themselves with normal, decent, socially acceptable language. This is easily remedied by study, and by observation of those who express themselves well with polite and pure words.

There is a lack of inner strength. Some use filthy words to appear "tough." In their vain attempt, some repulse even the wicked with their non-stop obscenities.

There is a lack of self-esteem. Some want so badly to be accepted, they will do whatever it takes. If the crowd one considers to be "cool," uses profanity, so will he. What a sad reason to sell one's soul!

There is a problem of habitual use. Those who have broken the habit of using filthy, corrupt words state that it was not easy. It becomes a way of life, and it is like a cancer that intertwines itself around the brain, whose removal is difficult at best. It is there and often goes unnoticed by the speaker.

There is the problem of using euphemisms, which is just another way, considered less offensive by some, of using corrupt communication. Guy N. Woods accurately presented the nature of this problem.

> Jehovah has ever regarded, with the greatest displeasure, any disposition on the part of man to use his name in flippant, frivolous and profane fashion....One is profane who uses sacred things in an irreverent and a blasphemous manner. The word vain, in the third commandment of the decalogue, is translated from a word which means in a light, flippant, and contemptuous fashion. It is of serious consequence that many members of the church have allowed to creep into their phraseology words and phrases the use of which amounts to profanity. Others, who would not dare use the holy names of God, Christ, Jesus, Jerusalem, Heaven, Hell, hades, as interjections ("An ejaculatory word or form of speech, usually thrown in without grammatical connection" Webster), and for emphasis, will nevertheless use euphemisms

> (the substitution of a word or a phrase less offensive or objectionable), the derivation of which goes back to one of the foregoing forms. Were those who thus do aware of the origin of many of these common by-words they would be shocked! It is therefore important that we obtain a clear conception of the significance of such words and phrases and avoid all which even directly border on the profane.[13]

Brother Woods then lists several euphemisms including Gee Whiz, Gosh, Gad, Egad, Golly, Good Gracious, Good Grief, Goodness, Heavens, Good Heavens, For Heaven's Sake, etc.[14] Once, while standing in a lunch line at a lectureship, a member of the church used a shocking euphemism. As I pondered how best to approach this brother, a little girl, the daughter of a preacher friend, did far more than I ever could. She immediately spoke up and said, "You ought not to use bad words in front of the preacher's girl." What a great sermon--and one that, I am sure, he has never forgotten!

Lying and corrupt communication are repulsive and disgusting to all who renounce "ungodliness and worldly lusts," and who would "live soberly, righteously, and godly, in this present world" (Tit. 2:12).

THE SOLUTION TO THIS SIN

Repent of evil communication. Lying and corrupt communication are sins; thus, bring condemnation, and demand repentance (Rom. 6:23; Acts 17:30-31). One, far too easily, can fall into the habit of impure speech. Some are so in the habit of lying they lie when there is, seemingly, no reason to lie. God commands us: "Wherefore putting away lying, speak every man truth with his neighbour: for we are members one of another" (Eph. 4:25). Repentance may require restitution (to the point possible, cf. Luke 19:8). Repentance also requires renouncing former sins (2 Cor. 4:2).

In addition, we must get away from evil influences that "corrupt good morals" (1 Cor. 15:33). The key to avoiding corrupt communication is to cleanse the mind and keep it pure. Think on things that are true, honest, just, pure, lovely, of good report, virtuous, and praise worthy (Phi. 4:8; Pro. 23:7; Mat. 12:34). Then, practice kind, considerate, truthful, uplifting speech. Use sound (healthy), wholesome communication that does good and not evil.

Receive the truth. Knowing it is wrong to receive a lie or impure words, do not receive (do not listen to) improper speech. If one does not listen to it, he will not be able to repeat it. Listening to the deceitful tales of the ungodly who are wrapped up in worldliness is wrong and condemns the listener as wicked! “A wicked doer giveth heed to false lips; and a liar giveth ear to a naughty tongue” (Pro. 17:4). Jesus warned: “Take heed that no man deceive you” (Mat. 24:4; cf. 5, 11, 24). “He that worketh deceit shall not dwell within my house: he that telleth lies shall not tarry in my sight” (Psa. 101:7). We are to love truth (Pro. 23:23), and we are to hate lying (Pro. 13:15).

Repeat the truth. Knowing it is wrong to tell what is false or unbecoming a Christian's speech, we must tell what is true and pure. "These are the things that ye shall do; speak ye every man the truth to his neighbour; execute the judgment of truth and peace in your gates" (Zec. 8:16). We must use, "Sound speech, that cannot be condemned; that he that is of the contrary part may be ashamed, having no evil thing to say of you" (Tit. 2:8; cf. Mat. 5:37). Jesus spoke true and pure words (Mark 12:14), and we are to follow His perfect example (1 Pet. 2:21). Seeking to avoid blame by saying, "I am just repeating what someone told me," does not absolve one of guilt (Pro. 11:13). "Where no wood is, there the fire goeth out: so where there is no talebearer, the strife ceaseth. As coals are to burning coals, and wood to fire; so is a contentious man to kindle strife" (Pro. 26:20-21; cf. Rom. 1:28-32). "He that covereth a transgression seeketh love; but he that repeateth a matter separateth very friends" (Pro. 17:9).

Respect the truth. How? By receiving truth, and refusing evil. By respecting oneself, one's neighbor, and God. By exhibiting Christian love and Godly courage. How long will the man of corrupt, lying lips continue when his listeners condemn his wickedness, call upon him to repent, and turn away in disgust if he continues?

Rejoice in truth and purity of speech. Love rejoices in the truth (1 Cor. 13:6).

THE BLESSINGS OF PUTTING AWAY UNBECOMING, UNGODLY BEHAVIOR

Improper speech is a sin against oneself, against society, and against God. It robs man of that which is most valuable: hope of salvation, peace of mind, reputation, self-respect, happiness, opportunities to teach others, and Heaven as well. Putting away the sins of the tongue prevents the tragedies listed above, and promotes one in every right way, fitting him for fellowship with God now and eternally. One who is pure and right in speech does not fear a scrutiny of his words. "But he that doeth truth cometh to the light, that his deeds may be made manifest, that they are wrought in God" (John 3:21).

It is easier to tell the truth than to try to be consistent in lying. Sin will find one out. Nebuchadnezzar found out his "wise men" had been deceiving him.

But if ye will not make known unto me the dream, there is but one decree for you: for ye have prepared lying and corrupt words to speak before me, till the time be changed: therefore tell me the dream, and I shall know that ye can shew me the interpretation thereof (Dan. 2:9).

The truth is that one must tell a second lie to cover the first, and a third to cover the second, etc. (cf. Mark 14:66-72).

Do you want to live where men are truthful? Be truthful. Do you want to live where speech is pure? Use pure speech.

CONCLUSION

"Hold your tongue!" was the mother's rebuke to her young son. He tried, literally, to do what Mom said, but soon cried out, "It is too slippery." We must hold our slippery tongues. We must think before we speak, for, truly, our souls are at stake. The Psalmist said, "I will take heed to my ways, that I sin not with my tongue: I will keep my mouth with a bridle, while the wicked is before me" (Psa. 39:1).

A good man out of the good treasure of the heart bringeth forth good things: and an evil man out of the evil treasure bringeth forth evil things. But I say unto you, That every idle word that men shall speak, they shall give account thereof in the day of judgment. For by thy words thou shalt be justified, and by thy words thou shalt be condemned (Mat. 12:35-37).

"Death and life are in the power of the tongue: and they that love it shall eat the fruit thereof" (Pro. 18:21).

STUDY QUESTIONS

1. Show, from Scripture, God's attitude toward lying.
2. Who told the first lie? Where? When? Why?
3. According to statistics cited, how many Americans "lie regularly"?
4. List the reasons given why some lie. What other reasons might you suggest?
5. What is "corrupt communication"?
6. What are some of the reasons people use corrupt communication?
7. Define "euphemism," and tell why using euphemisms is wrong.
8. What can one do to cease using corrupt communication and lying words?
9. Against whom does one sin when he uses improper speech?
10. Show from the Scriptures where liars will be eternally.

ENDNOTES

1. B. C. Goodpasture, "Putting Away Falsehood," Gospel Advocate, 14 March 1940, p. 244.

2. Ibid.

3. Oliver Wendell Holmes, "The Autocrat of the Breakfast-Table," Chapter 6, Atlantic Monthly, 1858, available from http://eldred.ne.mediaone.net/owh/abt06.html.

4. Greg Laurie, "The Ten Commandments Part VI," Foundations for Living, http://www.harvest.org/tools/ffl/comand6.html; Internet.

5. Ibid.

6. Goodpasture, p. 244.

7. The Catholic Encyclopedia, IX, 471, as quoted in O. C. Lambert, Roman Catholicism Against Itself (Winfield, AL: O. C. Lambert, 1956), p. 72.

8. The Catholic Encyclopedia, X, 195 as quoted in Lambert, p.73.

9. Man. of Mor. Theol., I, 171-172, as quoted in Lambert, p. 73.

10. Thomas Aquinas, Summa Theologica , Second Part of the Second Part, Question 110, Article 2, trans. Fathers of the English Dominican Province,http://www.newadvent.org/summa/311002.htm; Internet.

11. Theodore Roosevelt, "The Strenuous Life VII--The Eighth and Ninth Commandments in Politics," Outlook, 12 May

1990, as quoted in Gary W. Summers, Spiritual Perspectives, 28 February, 1999, p. 3.

12. The Reagan Information Interchange, http://www.reagan.com/HotTopics.main/HotMike/document-12.2.1998.6.html; Internet.

13. Guy N. Woods, Questions and Answers OPEN FORUM (Nashville: Freed-Hardeman College, 1976, pp. 180-181.

14. Ibid., pp. 181-183.

MARRIAGE AND DIVORCE

Larry Yarber

INTRODUCTION [1]

The theme for this year's lectures is "MORALS IN AN IMMORAL AGE." Webster defines moral;

> moral, mor-al, … of or concerned with the principles of right and wrong in conduct and character; teaching or upholding standards of good behavior; conforming to the rules of right conduct; sexually virtuous; … capable of distinguishing between right and wrong; … ethics; principles and mode of life; behavior as to right or wrong, esp. in relation to sexual matters, p. 621 [2]

Although neither word, "moral" nor "immoral," appear in the KJV of the Bible, there is no doubt the Bible calls upon Christians to live moral lives and condemns all who practice immorality. Paul penned,

> Know ye not that the unrighteous shall not inherit the kingdom of God? Be not deceived, neither fornicators, nor idolaters, nor adulterers, nor effeminate, nor abusers of themselves with mankind, Nor thieves, nor covetous, nor drunkards, nor revilers, nor extortioners shall inherit the kingdom of God (1 Cor. 6:9-10).

AN IMMORAL AGE

Man has always had the tendency to look unto himself, instead of unto his Creator, for the answers to life's challenges. The wise man said, "There is a way which seemeth right unto a man; but the end thereof are the ways of death" (Prov. 14:12). In so doing, he brings upon himself both physical and spiritual ruin. Well did Jeremiah state, "O Lord, I know that the way of man is not in himself: it is not in man that walketh to direct his steps" (Jer. 10:23). In spite of God's wise admonitions, society after society has ignored these warnings only to suffer the consequences of their own foolish pride. Twice, toward the end of the book of Judges we are told, "In those days there was no king in Israel, but every man did that which was right in his own eyes", and, "In those days there was no king in Israel: every man did that which was right in his own eyes" (Judges 17:6;21:25). When man chooses to ignore the counsel of God and to seek after his own counsel, he has become guilty of setting himself above God, "Let no man deceive you by any means: for that day shall not come, except there come a falling away first, and that man of sin be revealed, the son of perdition; who opposeth and exalteth himself above all that is called God, or that is worshipped; so that he as God sitteth in the temple of God, shewing himself that he is God" (2 Thess. 2:3-4). As a society, we have reached this point. We readily accept divorce and seek to redefine marriage. Noah Webster, in an older dictionary (copyright 1973, 1972, 1971), defined marriage, "The social institution by which a man and woman are legally united and establish a new family unit; … the relation between husband and wife …" p. 584.[3] On June 29, 2008, answers.com defined marriage, "… The legal union of a man and woman as husband and wife, and in some jurisdictions, between two person of the same sex, …".[4] When men become so self deluded they reject even that which God reveals unto them through nature, nothing is left but for man to face the wrath of God, "For the wrath of God is revealed from heaven against all ungodliness and unrighteousness of men, who hold the truth in unrighteousness; Because that which may be known of God is manifest in them; for God hath shewed it unto them".

For this cause God gave them up unto vile affections: for even their women did change the natural use into that which is against nature: And likewise also the men, leaving the natural use of the woman, burned in their lusts one toward another; men with men working that which is unseemly, and receiving in themselves that recompense of their error which was meet (Rom. 1:18-19;26-27).

Sadly, our societal decay has flowed over into the church. Paul admonished the Roman Christians,

> I beseech you therefore, brethren, by the mercies of God, that ye present your bodies a living sacrifice, holy, acceptable unto God, which is your reasonable service. And be not conformed to this world: but be ye transformed by the renewing of your mind, that ye may prove what is that good, and acceptable, and perfect will of God (Rom. 12:1-2).

Yet, many who profess Christianity have allowed themselves to be formed into the same image as those in the world. Peter said these individuals have adulterous eyes, and are as sexually unrestrained as the brute beast of the field, and who will bring upon themselves swift destruction and on all others who listen to and follow their damnable heresies,

> But there were false prophets also among the people, even as there shall be false teachers among you, who privily shall bring in damnable heresies, even denying the Lord that bought them, and bring upon themselves swift destruction. And many shall follow their pernicious ways; … (2 Pet. 2:1-2).

> But these, as natural brute beasts, made to be taken and destroyed, speak evil of the things that they understand not; and shall utterly perish in their own corruption; and shall receive the reward of unrighteousness, as they that count it pleasure to riot in the daytime. …Having eyes full of adultery, and that cannot cease from sin; … (2 Pet. 2:12-14).

Not only does God hold individuals responsible for their immoral behavior, but as we previously noted, He also holds nations accountable for their loose morals in the here and now. If only ten righteous had been found in Sodom and Gomorrah, it would still be standing today, "And he said, Oh let not the Lord be angry, and I will speak yet but this once: Peradventure ten shall be found there. And he said, I will not destroy it for ten's sake" (Gen. 18:32). The land of Canaan was annihilated by God through the sword of Israel because of her immorality,

> Moreover thou shalt not lie carnally with thy neighbor's wife, to defile thyself with her. … Thou shalt not lie with mankind, as with womankind: it is abomination. Neither shalt thou lie with any beast … neither shall any woman stand before a beast to lie down thereto: it is confusion. … (For all these abominations have the men of the land done, which were before you, and the land is defiled;) That the land spue not you out also, when ye defile it, as it spued out the nations that were before you (Lev. 18:20-28).

> For thus saith the Lord God; How much more when I send my four sore judgments upon Jerusalem, the sword, and the famine, and the noisome beast, and the pestilence, to cut off from it man and beast (Ezek. 14:21).

Concerning this judgment of God by the sword of Israel against the land of Canaan, brother James Burton Coffman writes;

> This army of Israel which slaughtered these kings and all of their subjects was actually one of the most terrible military forces ever to appear in human history. They took no prisoners, but slaughtered man, woman, and child without mercy. They did this, of course, by divine orders; and, in this, we are able to

> read the utter abhorrence in which God beholds sin, p. 32.[5]

Our last example is the washing of the world in the days of the flood. We must remember that it was not God's intention to bring a complete end to the world at this time. If He had done this, the salvation of all men throughout all time would have been forfeited, for the Savior who would eventually cleanse the world of her sin had not yet come. But this judgment was so great and horrific that it would change the climatic atmosphere of the earth forever, as well as the lifestyle and lifespan of all humankind.

> And God saw that the wickedness of man was great in the earth, and that every imagination of the thoughts of his heart was only evil continually. And it repented the Lord that he had made man on the earth, and it grieved him at his heart. And the Lord said, I will destroy man whom I have created from the face of the earth; both man and beast, and the creeping thing, and the fowls of the air; for it repenteth me that I have made them. But Noah found grace in the eyes of the Lord (Gen. 6:5-8).

Had it not been for these eight righteous souls, the earth may have come to an end at this time. Furthermore, it is the righteous of earth today which stands between God and earth's final judgment. When they lose their influence for good, not only will nations fall in judgment, but the entire world in which we live, "Ye are the salt of the earth: but if the salt hath lost his savour, wherewith shall it be salted? it is thenceforth good for nothing, but to be cast out, and to be trodden under foot of men" (Matt. 5:13). It is imperative to the salvation of all men that a moral society be maintained so the lost will have the opportunity to hear and obey God before they pass into eternal consequences.

MARRIAGE AND DIVORCE

"Marriage is honorable in all, and the bed undefiled: but whoremongers and adulterers God will judge" (Heb. 13:4).

Marriage did not evolve through time and societal custom as propagated by intellects of today. Marriage was ordained of God from creation;

> And the Lord God said, It is not good that the man should be alone; I will make him a help meet for him. And out of the ground the Lord God formed every beast of the field, and every fowl of the air; and brought them unto Adam to see what he would call them: and whatsoever Adam called every living creature, that was the name thereof. And Adam gave names to all cattle, and to the fowl of the air, and to every beast of the field; but for Adam there was not found a help meet for him. And the Lord God caused a deep sleep to fall upon Adam, and he slept: and he took one of his ribs, and closed up the flesh instead thereof; and the rib, which the Lord God had taken from man, made he a woman, and brought her unto the man. And Adam said, This is now bone of my bones, and flesh of my flesh: she shall be called Woman, because she was taken out of Man. Therefore shall a man leave his father and his mother, and shall cleave unto his wife: and they shall be one flesh (Gen. 2:18-24).

Let's note several facts that can be learned about marriage in all of the above.

First, any sexual relationship outside of the marital realm is wrong and those who engage in this type of immoral behavior will be condemned by God. In order to escape the condemnation, Paul admonished those at Corinth, "Nevertheless, to avoid fornication, let every man have his own wife, and let every woman have her own husband" (1 Cor. 7:2). Here we find one of at least three purposes for the marital realm: One is to fulfill the intimate passion of man, as stated above (1 Cor. 7:2). Second, when God saw that it was not good for man to be alone, He created a lifelong companion for man. Thus, the second purpose of marriage is companionship (Gen. 2:18). Thirdly, the marital realm is for reproduction, "And God blessed them, and God said unto them, Be fruitful, and multiply, and replenish the earth, and subdue it: and have dominion over the fish of the sea, and over the fowl of the air, and over every living thing that moveth upon the earth" (Gen. 1:28).

God intended marriage to be between a man and a woman. Any other intimate relationship was strictly forbidden. The parade of the various animals of the earth before Adam revealed the beasts were not suitable companions for man. To fornicate with a beast is abominable unto God, "Neither shalt thou lie with any beast to defile thyself therewith: neither shall any woman stand before a beast to lie down thereto: it is confusion" (Lev. 18:23). Nor did God create another man for Adam. This, too, is abominable before God, "Thou shalt not lie with mankind, as with womankind: it is abomination" (Lev. 18:22). Since Paul had said above, "… let every man have his own wife, and let every woman have her own husband" (1 Cor. 7:2), it is just as plain to see women are not suitable companions for women. This, too, is abominable in the sight of God!

It is just as clear, that from the beginning, God intended for this bond to exist until the death of one of the spouses.

> The Pharisees also came unto him, tempting him, and saying unto him, Is it lawful for a man to put away his wife for every cause? And, he answered and said unto them, Have ye not read, that he which made them at the beginning made them male and female, And said, For this cause shall a man leave father and mother, and shall cleave to his wife: and they twain shall be one

> flesh? Wherefore they are no more twain, but one flesh. What therefore God hath joined together, let not man put asunder. They say unto him, why did Moses then command to give a writing of divorcement, and to put her away? He saith unto them, Moses because of the hardness of your hearts suffered you to put away your wives: but from the beginning it was not so. And I say unto you, whosoever shall put away his wife, except it be for fornication, and shall marry another, committeth adultery: and whoso marrieth her which is put away doth commit adultery (Matt. 19:3-9).

Again, let's note some lessons we can learn from all of the above.

First, a husband/wife is bound to their spouse until death. In the case of fornication, the innocent party can set aside their spouse and remarry.

> For the woman which hath a husband is bound by the law to her husband so long as he liveth; but if the husband be dead, she is loosed from the law of her husband (Rom. 7:2). It hath been said, whosoever shall put away his wife, let him give her a writing of divorcement: But I say unto you, That whosoever shall put away his wife, saving for the cause of fornication, causeth her to commit adultery: and whosoever shall marry her that is divorced committeth adultery (Matt. 5:31-32).

In the case of death, the surviving spouse is free to remarry,

> So then if, while her husband liveth, she be married to another man, she shall be called an adulteress: but if her husband be dead, she is free from that law; so that she is no adulteress, though she be married to another man" (Rom. 7:3).

Please note, if she remarries while her husband still lives, she is now an adulterous. The only way one can be forgiven of sin is to depart from sin. Thus, to be forgiven, she must set aside this adulterous union. Also, note in the previously quoted passage (Matt. 5:31-32), the exception to the rule only applies to the innocent party. The guilty is not given the freedom to remarry.

In an attempt to set aside what God had joined together, two false doctrines are advanced to annul the above. One is called the "Pauline Privilege" and comes from a misinterpretation of 1 Corinthians 7:15,

> And the woman which hath a husband that believeth not, and if he be pleased to dwell with her, let her not leave him. …But if the unbelieving depart, let him depart. A brother or a sister is not under bondage in such cases: but God hath called us to peace" (1 Cor. 7:13-15).

Three verses prior to this statement, Paul had told the wife not to depart from her husband, but if she did, she was to remain unmarried or to be reconciled to him,

> And unto the married I command, yet not I, but the Lord, let not the wife depart from her husband: But and if she depart, let her remain unmarried, or be reconciled to her husband: and let not the husband put away his wife (1 Cor. 7:10-11).

It is absurd to think that one verse later, he would completely annul what he had just said three verses earlier. All Paul is saying is the marital bond does not trump our bondage to Christ. If it comes to the point of faithfulness to Christ or faithfulness to the marriage, Christ must be first. Lipscomb and Shepherd wrote concerning these passages;

The meaning is most likely that the believer can regard the unbelievers act as final, and need not to seek to live with him, while yet in such cases remarriage is not approved. The Christian should be prepared to restore the marriage relation when possible, and this certainly is safe ground. If, however, the unbeliever should marry another person, he would by the act commit adultery and in that case the wife or husband would be at liberty to marry (p. 102). [6]

To this we add the scholarship of brother Max Patterson;

> The word bound is not the word used for the marriage bond. The word used here is douloo, a subject, a slave. Of the 133 times used in the New Testament, this word never refers to marriage. The word used for the marriage bond is deo, (Rom. 7:2: also 1 Cor. 7:27, 39- glued to, tie, bind). …Paul is saying the Christian is not enslaved to God because of his teaching on marriage in such a way that he would have to give up his allegiance to Christ in order to maintain the marriage. It is a mistake to assume that the departing unbeliever has broken the marriage bond, and that, therefore, one is free from that marriage. Desertion does not break this bond" pp. 52,53. [7]

The other false doctrine men seek to use to change our Lord's teaching on this subject is that the gospel records are part of the Old Testament and not applicable to us today. However, the Bible says Jesus came preaching the gospel of the kingdom, not the gospel of Judaism, "Now after that John was put in prison, Jesus came into Galilee, preaching the gospel of the kingdom of God" (Mark 1:14). Furthermore, the Hebrew writer states our salvation began with the teachings of Jesus Christ, "How shall we escape if we neglect so great salvation; which at the first began to be spoken by the Lord, and was confirmed unto us by them that heard him;" (Heb. 2:3). In John chapter three, Jesus taught the new birth, Christian baptism; in John chapter four, He taught of a new place and manner of worship,

Christian worship; and in Matthew chapter nineteen, He is stating His law on marriage and divorce, "And I say unto you, …" (Matt. 19:9). In verses four through six of this same book and chapter, He rehearses what was taught by God in the patriarchal age. In verses 7 and 8, He tells them what Moses taught on this matter. The gospel accounts are New Testament law and are applicable to us today.

Despite all God has said about marriage and divorce, man has no problem setting aside what God has joined together. The National Health Statistics Report of March 22, 2012, Number 49 states;

Current estimates of divorce indicate that about half of first marriages end in divorce" (2,3). [8]

From these divorced homes come the following alarming statistics; Fatherless homes account for 63% of youth suicides, 90% of homeless/runaway children, …85% of youth in prison, well over 50% of teen mothers. [9]

God's strong warning will ever stand, "…What therefore God hath joined together, let not man put asunder" (Matt. 19:6).

FIDELITY IN MARRIAGE

> My people are destroyed for lack of knowledge: because thou hast rejected knowledge, I will also reject thee, that thou shalt be no priest to me: seeing thou has forgotten the law of thy God, I will also forget thy children (Hosea 4:6). For Ezra had prepared his heart to seek the law of the Lord, and to do it, and to teach in Israel statutes and judgment (Ezra 7:10).

Education is one of the first steps toward freedom. Jesus said, "And ye shall know the truth, and the truth shall make you free" (John 8:32). Someone else has said, "Ignorance enslaves but truth empowers us". These are all true statements. The early apostasy of

Israel after the conquest transpired because they had failed to teach their children about God and all His wondrous works, "And also all that generation were gathered unto their fathers: and there arose another generation after them, which knew not the Lord, nor yet the works he had done for Israel" (Judges 2:10). One of the contributing factors to the success of the early church's growth, as well as to the growth of immorality today, was/is education. The high priest of the Jewish Sanhedrin Court exclaimed, "Saying, Did not we straightly command you that ye should not teach in this name? and, behold, ye have filled Jerusalem with your doctrine, and intend to bring this man's blood upon us" (Acts 5:28). Today, through the public Educational System and media, our children are "filled" with the doctrines of Atheism, Humanism, Modernism, etc., while we have been relegated to teaching God's word in the church building behind closed doors. As a result, our children now speak the language of the world instead of the language of God, "In those days also saw I Jews that had married wives of Ashdod, of Ammon, and of Moab: And their children spake half in the speech of Ashdod, and could not speak in the Jews language, but according to the language of each people" (Neh. 13:23-24). Fathers and mothers are supposed to raise their children in the nurture and admonition of the Lord, and not in the way of Satan and of the world, "And ye fathers, provoke not your children to wrath: but bring them up in the nurture and admonition of the Lord" (Eph. 6:4). "I will therefore that the younger women marry, bear children, guide the house, …" (1 Tim. 5:14). Until we step out of the church building and "fill" Jerusalem with the doctrine of Christ, society is going to continue to trample under foot the sacred institutions of God, such as marriage.

Ezra was a doer of the law before he became a teacher. So was our Lord, "The former treatise have I made, O Theophilus, of all that Jesus began both to do and teach" (Acts 1:1). Paul asked,

> Thou therefore which teachest another, teachest thou not thyself? Thou that preacheth a man should not

> steal, dost thou steal? Thou that sayest a man should not commit adultery, dost thou commit adultery? thou that abhorrest idols, dost thou commit sacrilege? Thou that makest thy boast of the law, through breaking the law dishonourest thou God? For the name God is blasphemed among the Gentiles through you, as it is written (Rom. 2:21-24).

Failure to practice what we preach annuls the sermon of our life. Furthermore, when our own marital relationship is not in harmony with God's teachings on marriage and the home, our own spiritual relationship with God is jeopardized, "Likewise, ye husbands, dwell with them according to knowledge, giving honor unto the wife, as unto the weaker vessel, and as being heirs together of the grace of life; that your prayers be not hindered" (1 Pet. 3:7). We should enter into marriage with every intention of holding marriage together until death. One way to achieve this goal is to pick a proper spouse. While it may not be a sin to marry a non-Christian, it is certainly unwise. Paul warned, "Be not deceived, evil communications corrupt good manners" (1 Cor. 15:33).

It behooves the woman to remember men are more physically inclined and, therefore, the intimate relationship in marriage is probably more significant to him than the emotional (1 Cor. 7:3). Therefore, the wife should give heed to her attractiveness in order to keep her husband's desires satisfied. Women, on the other hand, are more interested in an emotional relationship than the man. Therefore, the husband needs to provide this emotional support for his wife lest she become discouraged and unsatisfied in the marriage (Gen. 2:18). Neglect by either party in these realms can lead to serious problems within the marriage.

Before Ezra was a teacher, he was a doer. And, before he was a doer, he was a learner. Before entering into the marital state, a person needs to conduct a thorough study of a man's role in marriage and the home, and a woman's role in marriage and the home. Too many men believe to rule the house simply means to be the boss and too many women believe to guide the house simply means to give birth and drop the kids off with the babysitter. A man has two roles in the home if there are children in the family. He is both a father and a husband. He is to rule in a dignified manner, "One that ruleth well his own house, having his children in subjection with all gravity;" (1 Tim. 3:4). Gravity here means; "semnotes, sem-not-ace; from 4586 semnos; vulnerableness, i.e. probity: - gravity, honesty" (STRONG, p. 65). [10]

This means he does not rule as a bully but in an honorable manner. Likewise, he is to provide for the home, "But if any provide not for his own and specially for those of his own house, he hath denied the faith, and is worse than an infidel" (1 Tim. 5:8). In a house where children are present, women also have two roles to fulfill. They are both a wife and a mother. To guide the home is to give that home direction and purpose, "I will therefore that the younger women marry, bear children, guide the house…" (1 Tim. 5:14). Even after the children have left the nest, husbands and wives still have obligations to the home which should not be neglected.

Finally, we have an obligation and/or responsibility to society as a whole. As we noted earlier, Christianity and righteousness is the preservative of the earth (Matt. 5:13). These two things are all that stand between God and the judgment of sinful nations. When that influence is gone, God will judge the nation/world. It has been said, and I believe, rightfully so, that with opportunity and ability come responsibility, "For if there be first a willing mind, it is accepted according to that a man hath, and not according to that he hath not" (1 Cor. 9:12). "As we have therefore opportunity, let us do good unto all men, especially unto them who are of the household of faith" (Gal. 6:10). We have been given a unique opportunity in America, through the power of the vote, to change the course of society, and to preserve it for subsequent generations. We are not trying to persuade anyone to vote Republican or Democrat, or for any other party. We are just trying to exhort our fellow man to vote in such a manner as to stop the onslaught of evil upon morality. If we do not, the next generation may not be here. The old adage, "morality cannot be legislated" is false to the core. In the name of morality, murder is condemned by almost every society. Stealing, likewise, is condemned. So, while we are not trying to force anyone to adhere to a particular religion, we do insist that mankind maintain laws holding society accountable for practicing immorality which even nature itself declares to be wrong.

CONCLUSION

"…Therefore, take heed to your spirit, and let none deal treacherously against the wife of his youth. "For the Lord, the God of Israel, saith that he hateth putting away: …" (Mal. 2:15-16). Man has no right nor authority to tamper with the divine institution of marriage which was established by God from the beginning of the world. With all the events unfolding in the world of today, we need to do all we can to make sure God's moral laws stand for the next generation. Failure to do so will lead to the judgment and fall of our own nation, if not the world, and eventually the spiritual demise of all who ignore God's moral laws. May we close this study with this thought, "…What therefore God hath joined together, let not man put asunder" (Matt. 19:6).

STUDY QUESTIONS

1. Define marriage in the eyes of God.
2. Are nations held accountable in the here and now for their immoral behavior?
3. Give three examples of the above.
4. Did marriage originate and evolve from man or was it divinely instituted by God in the Garden of Eden?
5. List three purposes found in the marital realm.
6. List four sexual perversions which are abominable to God.
7. What are the two privileges granting a subsequent marriage?
8. Explain the "so-called" Pauline Privilege.
9. Are the gospel accounts, (Matthew, Mark, Luke, John), part of the New Testament or part of the Old Testament?
10. Who, or what, is the preservative of the earth?

WORKS CITED

1. All scripture quotations taken from the KJV of the Bible unless otherwise noted.

2. The Living Webster Encyclopedia of the English Language, Noah Webster, The English Language Institute of America Inc., Chicago, Illinois, 1973, (p. 621).

3. The Living Webster Encyclopedia of the English Language, Noah Webster, The English Language Institute of America Inc., Chicago, Illinois, 1973, (p. 584).

4. http://www.answers.com/topic/marriage 6-19-12.

5. James Burton Coffman Commentaries, Deuteronomy, Volume 4, A-C-U Press, 1988, (p.32).

6. A Commentary on the New Testament Epistle, David Lipscomb and J. W. Shepherd, Volume II, First Corinthians, Gospel Advocate Company, Nashville, Tenn., 1979, p. 102.

7. An Outline Commentary on First Corinthians, Max Patterson, 2004, pgs. 52-53.

8. http://www.cdc.gov/nchs/data/nhsr/nhsr049.pdf - National Health Statistics Report, Number 49, March 22, 2012.

9. http://www.divorcemag.com/statistics/statsUS2 - US Divorce Statistics.

10. The Exhaustive Concordance of the Bible, James Strong, McDonald Publishing Company, McLean, Virginia, (pgs. 419 and 65)

SEXUAL IMMORALITY

Melvin L. Otey

INTRODUCTION

Circumspect saints will generally agree that American society has an alarming problem with sexual immorality. But, perhaps Christians have become somewhat desensitized to the magnitude of the trouble because it is so incredibly pervasive. We live in an age of highly-public "wardrobe malfunctions," "sexting," and "Girls Gone Wild" foolishness. Various elements in our culture affirmatively promote a lifestyle of careless physical intimacy, even early in one's dating life. Today, the idea of remaining chaste until marriage is popularly dismissed as archaic and prude.

Most scarcely remember that people were once ashamed to become parents or romantically cohabitate without first being married. Sadly, younger generations have never even known such times. One-third of all children born in 2000 were out-of-wedlock (Crawford 84), and "shacking up" has become so commonplace that people are formalizing their sinful living arrangements with legal contracts called "cohabitation agreements" (Dickler). However, no matter how comfortable the world becomes with sexual sin, God's people should have a true sense of distress about it because, among other reasons, all sin grieves our God (Gen. 6:6).

THE SITUATION REGARDING SEXUAL IMMORALITY

To the extent that Christians could ever become comfortable with the reality that our society is infested with sexual immorality, one should nevertheless be startled by the rapid exacerbation of the problem. More than simply being bad, the situation is getting dramatically and demonstrably worse.

Consider, for example, the current epidemic concerning pornography. With the explosion of computers and the internet, clandestine access to pornography has exploded as well. Voyeurism is big business now; revenue from the pornography industry in the United States actually exceeds the combined revenues of ABC, CBS, and NBC (Ropelato).

As of 2006, 12% of all web sites were pornographic in content, 25% of all search engine requests were for pornography, the average age of first internet exposure to pornography was eleven, and 33% of visitors to "adult" websites were female. Moreover, the problem is not just "out there"; it is hitting close to home. Forty-seven percent of those who self-identify as Christians have indicated that pornography is a major problem in their homes (Ropelato). Until recent years, voyeurism was a vice commonly ascribed to "dirty old men" and curious, pubescent boys, but no one can credibly maintain such an optimistic fallacy today.

The ongoing paradigm shift in societal attitudes regarding homoerotic behavior also illustrates the degree to which the problem of sexual immorality is metastasizing. Only a few decades ago, the idea of homosexuality was taboo, only whispered about in dark corners. In recent years, however, it has been repackaged as a consequence of genetics, re-labeled an "alternative lifestyle," and promoted unabashedly and relentlessly across nearly all aspects of society. Entertainment programming and workplace "sensitivity training" encourage acceptance of homosexuality and, in some cases, homoerotic experimentation. The school systems are blinding young minds to the obvious fallacies of the behavior, churches that self-identify as "Christian" are publicly embracing it, and state and federal governments, which are tasked by God with restraining evil (Rom. 13:1-4), are sanctioning this specific brand of immorality through legislation and the court rulings.

The accompanying changes have been staggering. Open hostility has largely been replaced by shameless glorification. For example, in 2008, Katy Perry, a "former Christian-pop singer" reached the top of America's music charts with a homoerotic tune about kissing another girl (Reuters), Madonna seemingly cannot make a public appearance without kissing another female performer, and Lady Gaga, an openly homosexual singer, admits wanting to inject gay culture into the mainstream. The number of same-sex couples in the United States continues to rise, as does the number of same-sex couples raising children (Gomes 15). Things have changed so radically that those who speak against homoerotic behavior, even to raise a religious objection, risk discipline by their employers and being socially marginalized as "homophobic."

Decades of secularist, humanist, and relativist influences in our scholastic, entertainment, and political systems have taken a devastating toll, and the effects are as pronounced in general societal attitudes regarding sexuality as they are in any other aspect of life. Perhaps this is inevitable because, whenever sacred matters are broached without appreciation for God and His will, men inevitably miss the mark. In this case, we are missing it by a mile. We are on a "runaway train of unrestrained hedonism" (Young and Adams 87).

While pornography and homoeroticism are not particularly worse than other forms of sexual immorality in terms of their eternal consequences, the degree of their proliferation is illustrative of just how prurient people become when they walk away from God. As Wayne Jackson rightly observed, "Rebellion against Jehovah especially seems to express itself in the basest forms of sexual perversion" (Jackson 266).

THE SIGNIFICANCE OF SEXUAL IMMORALITY

While American society has an obvious and egregious problem with sexual immorality, America is not unique. Men have rather consistently fallen to fornication, almost since the beginning of time. In the antediluvian era, Lamech was guilty of adultery because he was married to two women at one time (Gen. 4:23). At a time when the thoughts of men's hearts were "only evil continually" (Gen. 6:5), it is hard to imagine that his fornication was a unique problem. The seedy episode between Judah and Tamar demonstrates that prostitution existed not later than the days of the patriarchs (Gen. 38). In the New Testament age, Paul reminded the Corinthian saints that they had formerly engaged in fornication of every kind, including adultery and homosexual intercourse (1 Cor. 6:9-11).

While human beings have rather continually persisted in sexual immorality, they have done so despite God's clear and intensely negative feelings toward such transgressions. He gave His written law specifically to restrain, among others, "whoremongers" (1 Tim. 1:8-10). Nearly every book in the Bible warns against fornication, which includes all sexual conduct involving an unmarried person (1 Cor. 7:2), all adulterous relationships (Lk. 16:18, 18:20; Ex. 20:14; Prov. 6:32), all homoerotic conduct (Rom. 1:24, 26-27; Gen. 19; Jude 7; Lev. 18:22), and even bestiality (Lev. 18:23). The Lord went so far as to condemn the unrestrained thought of such conduct (Mt. 5:28; Ex. 20:17).

The Bible speaks so decisively against sexual immorality, especially among Christians, because, in all its forms, it involves an abuse of God's property (1 Cor. 6:15). Christians are "bought with a price" (1 Cor. 6:20, 7:23). We belong to God and are duty-bound to use our bodies only in manners that He approves (Rom. 12:1; cf. Col. 3:17). Christ, who gave Himself as payment for our sin (1 Jn. 3:16; Rev. 5:8-9), would never approve of our engaging in sin of any kind, including sexual sin (1 Cor. 6:15). We do not have his permission to use our bodies in this fashion.

Sexual immorality is also wrong because it constitutes an abuse of God's design for physical intimacy (1 Cor. 6:16). He specifically designed sexual intercourse for the marriage relationship

(Gen. 1:27-28, 2:24; Mal. 2:15). When His design is respected, sex is intimate, holy, and beautiful (Heb. 13:4). When it is abused, it becomes "dirty" and shameful. Instead of something to celebrate, it becomes something to hide.

All fornication, then, is sinful (1 Thes. 4:3; 1 Jn. 3:4), and we are not left to guess about the grave consequences for such transgressions. In the short term, fornication begets sexually transmitted diseases, abortions, broken homes, degradation of the national morality, reproach for the Lord's church, and such like. However, inordinate focus on these temporary, yet weighty, consequences actually obscures the ultimate significance of the behavior.

Whatever one makes of the immediate consequences of fornication, and they are significant, the ultimate consequences should be far more frightening. God destroyed Sodom and several surrounding cities because the inhabitants were wholly given to sexual immorality, and He expects men and women today to learn from their mistakes (Gen. 19; Jude 1:7). Fornicators are among those who will endure God's wrath in eternity rather than inherit His kingdom (Col. 3:5-6; Rev. 21:8; 1 Cor. 6:9-10; Gal. 5:19-21; Eph. 3:3-5; cf. Dt. 22:22-24). There is simply no room in heaven for unrepentant fornicators.

THE SOLUTION FOR SEXUAL IMMORALITY

The situation is definitely bad, and it seems to be getting worse with each passing day. The problems are most dire, but the tide absolutely can be turned, at least for our lives, our homes, our congregations, and our communities. God calls us to "abstain from fornication" (1 Thes. 4:3); "mortify" the aspects of our being that produce fornication (Col. 3:5); and avoid walking "in orgies and drunkenness," "in sexual immorality and sensuality" (Rom. 13:13 ESV). He would not tell us to do something we are incapable of doing.

He expects us to maintain sexual purity because we can, but we need a sound plan for doing so and the faithful conviction to adhere to it.

Step #1: Recognize the Danger

In order to keep ourselves from fornication, we must first recognize the danger, because we are not typically motivated to avoid things we perceive as harmless. Sexual immorality carries a terrible cost. When we engage in sexual sins, we pay a price (see, e.g., 1 Cor. 5:3-5), our families pay a price (see, e.g., Mk. 10:11-12; Lk. 16:18), our congregations pay a price (see, e.g., 1 Cor. 5:6-7), and our nation pays a price (see, e.g., Prov. 14:34). Everyone pays. We must sincerely embrace what the Bible says about the dangers of sexual immorality and the design of sexual intimacy and be honest with ourselves about the harm.

We should learn from Job in this respect. He was faced with sensual temptation in his day, just as we contend with it today. Job, who was blameless and upright in his generation, one who feared God and shunned evil (Job 1:1), shared one of the keys to his success in remaining sexually pure: "I made a covenant with mine eyes; why then should I think upon a maid?" (Job 31:1). Like Job, we must recognize that even lustful leering is dangerous (Job 31:2-3). We can be blameless and upright in our generation also if we are as serious as Job about recognizing the dangers of fornication and steering clear of it.

Step #2: Reinforce the Boundaries

Second, having recognized the dangers, we must reinforce our boundaries. Fornication is never an accident, and it does not "just happen." At best, it is the result of reckless indifference, and, at worst, it is the result of base design. We would be at an understandable disadvantage if we could not know that temptation would beset us or, better yet, has beset us already. However, we are in a position to array our defenses and strengthen our boundaries so that sexual immorality will not be named among us (Eph. 5:3).

Daniel, for example, set boundaries to keep himself from embracing physical gratification to the point of sin. As a young man, the prophet was tempted with king's meats, "But Daniel purposed in his heart that he would not defile himself" (Dan. 1:8). We live in a similar environment, one that inundates us with the specter of physical gratification, and we must also fix our minds to do what God tells us is right. "The time to plant hedges is before the enemy attacks" (Jenkins 46).

If we are interested in someone romantically, we need to be circumspect about the environment in which we spend time with them. There is nothing lawful we can learn about them at midnight that we cannot learn at noon. If one is not married to the object of his interest, there is nothing he can do with her in private that he cannot lawfully do in public. We need sensible rules and guidelines for our protection and for the protection of those around us. Some precautions may seem excessive to the sex-crazed world we live in, but godly people do not "follow a multitude to do evil" (Ex. 23:2). It is a good idea to be different in this respect.

Appropriate, firm boundaries will help us avoid temptation. We will fail far more often than we should if we are not predetermined to say "No" and mean it (cf. Jam. 1:8; Mt. 5:37); avoid lustful thoughts and feast on wholesome thoughts (Phil. 4:8; Mt. 15:19), avoid corrupting influences and keep good company (1 Cor. 15:33), and walk circumspectly when using conveniences like the internet or even when cruising the malls (Rom. 12:9b; Eph. 5:15). Prospectively reinforcing our protective hedges is a vital key to maintaining sexually purity.

Step #3: Rally the Allies

Once we have reinforced our boundaries, we will need to rally our allies. We should not attempt to overcome struggles with fornication in isolation. Even if we are not currently struggling with pornography or adultery or impure thoughts, it is advisable to solicit aid from people of "like precious faith" who will strengthen us where and when we are weak (Prov. 27:17). Everyone has blind spots, and no one is so strong that he or she cannot fall into sexual impurity (1 Cor. 10:12).

Many times, people descend into fornication rather gradually. "Just as it's the little foxes that spoil the vine, so seemingly small indiscretions add up to major traps" (Jenkins 28). Accountability partners can help squelch an ungodly descent before it begins, or at least before it gains significant momentum. Regular gatherings with same-sex friends for encouragement can make a big difference. Even when things go too far and our boundaries are obliterated, a "brother's keeper" or "sister's keeper" can bring us back.

Remember David and Bathsheba. Neither was apparently looking for trouble, but they definitely found it. David seemed to be neglecting his duties as a king (2 Sam. 11:1). Bathsheba was bathing in the open, which demonstrated a lack of modesty (2 Sam. 11:2). When David saw her, instead of looking away as he should have, he inquired about her and pursued her (2 Sam. 11:3-4). The initial indiscretions of sloth and immodesty culminated in adultery, murder, and tremendous pain for their families and the nation, and David did not return to a godly path until Nathan confronted him (2 Sam. 1:1-13). It would have been far better for everyone if someone had been able to hold him accountable much sooner.

Inappropriate behavior can sometimes begin with seemingly innocent looks and touches. We need spiritually mature people who are willing to go beyond mere appearances, people we can trust to ask us the tough questions: "How would your husband feel if he heard you give that man that compliment? How do you think God feels about the way you just looked at that woman? Are you honoring your marital vows? Are you getting too close to that co-worker?" If we have struggled with viewing unsavory internet sites, we may need a service that will monitor our usage and share the results with accountability partners we designate.

Maybe these allies in our fight to maintain sexual purity can be empowered to bring our suspect behavior to the attention of others if, in their judgment, the concern is significant enough. "Fear of detection is not the most altruistic motive for avoiding such temptations, but use whatever works at the point of weakness" (Jenkins 80). In order to remain sexually pure, we need to summon allies who are willing to risk their friendship with us if that is required to protect our souls from sexual sin.

Step #4: Run!

Despite good boundaries and dependable allies, we will still come face-to-face with sensual temptation sometimes. One can hardly check his or her email account without encountering provocative photos of scantily clad men or shirtless, muscular men. Sales paper advertisements feature models wearing little more than is necessary to cover their reproductive organs, and there is no shortage of people who love pleasure more than they love God (cf. 2 Tim. 3:4). Temptation is all around us, and it will sometimes fall right in our laps, despite our best efforts.

As onerous as the temporal and eternal consequences are, it is difficult for many to resist fornication, partly because we often adopt the wrong strategy when our defenses are breached. We try to stand and resist. We try to stare down the enemy. But, the Bible does not instruct us to stand and fight. The Bible tells us to flee (1 Cor. 6:18a)! Paul's inspired instruction for remaining sexually pure is essentially this: "Run. Run like Jesse Owens. Run like Carl Lewis. Run like Ben Johnson on steroids. Run like Usain Bolt, and do not stop running until the coast is completely clear. Fly like the wind. Run, Forrest, run!"

Of course, there is no finer example of this truth than Joseph. He continually refused sexual advances from Potiphar's wife and even explained that he did not want to defraud Potiphar and sin against God by having a physical relationship with her (Gen. 39:6-

10). Yet, she became even more aggressive in her attempts to seduce him. Obviously, she was not a God-fearing woman. Joseph did not try to reason with her. He fled from her home so abruptly that he left his garment in her hand (Gen. 39:11-12).

There is no virtue in seeing just how far the other person is willing to go. There is nothing noble about testing our own limits to withstand sexual temptation. We do not need to be concerned about what others will think if we frankly end improper conversations or abruptly announce, “It’s time for me to leave.” When our boundaries are breached, we need to flee, and there is no need for apologies when doing so.

It is imperative that we do not deceive ourselves about our vulnerability to sexual immorality. David was a man after God’s own heart (Acts 13:22), and he fell. We are vulnerable. This is a battle we can lose. People lose it every day. In the end, we have to be prepared to retreat. Dramatic action is sometimes necessary to avoid being overtaken; it is better to run at the first than regret and repent, or even perish, at the last.

CONCLUSION

Our culture is increasingly emphasizing immediate sensual gratification, and our hearts are continually flooded with sensual images and avenues for carnal pursuits. We cannot wait for the world to change. Satan is generally having his way and will likely continue to have his way until Christ returns (cf. Eph. 2:1-3). His influence is manifest in all kinds of sexual immorality. Our families and our congregations are not immune to the problems this brings about. Therefore, we all need to be sober and vigilant about maintaining our purity and helping others do the same.

Satan would love for us to adopt a laissez faire, “everyone is doing it,” mentality, but we are not ignorant of his devices (2 Cor.

2:11). We know that apathy regarding sexual immorality, even the unrestrained thought of having intercourse with someone to whom we are not scripturally married, displeases our God and condemns souls. Therefore, we cannot bury our heads in the sand. We must be urgent and frank about discussing God's standards for sexual intercourse, the gross perversions so prominent in the world, and the steps we can take to protect ourselves, our families, and our congregations.

STUDY QUESTIONS

1. How does man's sexual immorality affect God?
2. What societal factors have led to Americans' shifting attitudes regarding sexual immorality?
3. In what respect is sexual immorality an abuse of God's property?
4. In what respect is sexual immorality an abuse of God's design?
5. What are some of the significant earthly consequences of sexual immorality?
6. What are the eternal consequences of sexual immorality?
7. What critical step did Job take to avoid sexual immorality?
8. How can we use boundaries to avoid sexual immorality?
9. What are the benefits of enlisting the help of fellow Christians in our effort to avoid sexual immorality?
10. When all else fails, what are we to do when faced with sexual temptation?

WORKS CITED

Crawford, Mark. "The Importance of Father." The Complete Parenting Book. Eds. David Stoop and Jan Stoop. Grand Rapids: Revell, 2004.

Dickler, Jessica. "Sign the Prenup, Skip the Wedding." Money. May 2012: 24.

Gomes, Charlene. "The Need for Full Recognition of Same-Sex Marriages," The Humanist. September/October 2003: 15-19.

Jackson, Wayne. A New Testament Commentary. Stockton: Christian Courier, 2011.

Jenkins, Jerry. Hedges. Wheaton: Crossway Books, 2005.

Reuters, "Katy Perry's 'I Kissed a Girl' Tops US Charts," 17 July 2008. <http.//www.reuters.com/articlePrint?articleId=

SN2629119320080626>.

Ropelato, Jerry. "Internet Pornography Statistics." 9 July 2012. <http://internet-filter-review.toptenreviews.com/internet-pornography-statistics.html>.

Young, Ben and Samuel Adams. The Ten Commandments of Dating. Nashville: Nelson, 1999.

Made in the USA
Monee, IL
03 April 2021

63685717R00106